HEINEMANN
NEW WINDMILLS

SIX SHAKESPEARE STORIES

Bassanio's quest for love means that his best friend looks set to lose his life, until the arrival of a talented lawyer . . .

Macbeth learns that one murder is never enough as he descends into spiralling evil to keep his first crime concealed.

The ancient feud between families has tragic consequences when Romeo falls in love with Juliet.

The most famous of Shakespeare's plays retold as short and easy-to-read stories. Exciting, intriguing, amusing, Shakespeare's plays are brought to life by Leon Garfield's ideal introduction to the greatest playwright ever known.

ABOUT THE AUTHOR

Leon Garfield was born in Brighton in 1921 and educated there. In World War II he joined the army and served in the Medical Corps for five years.

He now lives with his wife, children's novelist Vivien Alcock, and is a full-time writer.

Leon Garfield has won several awards for his writing and some of his books like *Smith* and *The Strange Affair of Adelaide Harris* have been televised

SIX
SHAKESPEARE
STORIES

LEON GARFIELD

HEINEMANN
NEW WINDMILLS

Heinemann is a imprint of Pearson Education Limited, a company incorporated in England
and Wales, having its registered office at Edinburg Gate, Harlow, Essex, CM20 2JE. Registered
company number: 872828

Heinemann is a registered trademark of Pearson Education Limited

First published in Great Britain by Victor Gollancz Ltd

First published as this edition in the New Windmill Series 1994

29

ISBN: 978 0 435124 24 3

British Library Cataloguing in Publication Data
for this title is available from the British Library

Cover ilustration by Kevin Jenkins

Typeset by CentraCet Limited, Cambridge
Printed in China (CTPS/29)

Contents

Contents

Twelfth Night

Before you hear of the shipwreck, you must know that, inland from its wild sea coast, Illyria was a green and golden land, of thatched cottages, neat as well-combed children, of gracious mansions, and the noble palacc of the Duke. Orsino was his name, and, before the shipwreck, he was fathoms deep in love with Olivia, a fair countess who dwelt nearby.

"If music be the food of love," he sighed, gazing through his windows towards the lady's house, "play on, give me excess of it . . ." and his lute-player bent low over his beribboned instrument and filled the air with song. But alas! What pleasure was there in a feast for only one? The lady would have nothing to do with him, nor, indeed, with any of his sex. That is, until the shipwreck. She was in mourning for a brother deceased, and had shut herself away in her mansion, and vowed to see no suitors for seven long years.

"What a plague means my niece to take the death of her brother thus?" complained her uncle, Sir Toby Belch, a fat bag of wind and merriment who lived in her house and floated between kitchen and cellar like a portly bubble in stained brocade. He himself had fetched his niece a suitor, a long, thin knight by name of Sir Andrew Aguecheek; but it had been to no avail. Nonetheless, Sir Andrew kept paying for Sir Toby's entertainment in the foolish hope of becoming his nephew. Though he always dressed

1

young, it was a case of stale wine in a new bottle. To be honest, the knight was old enough to know better, and too old to do it. But Sir Toby kept him in hopes, and he kept Sir Toby in drink; which seemed a fair exchange.

Then, one day, came a shipwreck. Far out at sea, a sudden and fearful tempest sprang up. Huge winds came boiling out of black clouds and tore sea and sky to shreds. A vessel, frail as paper, lifted, plunged, turned and tossed, until at last caught between two roaring walls of water, it cracked and split! Its cargo of shrieking souls was tumbled helplessly among the waves. Some clutched at spars and broken fragments of the mast, while others clung, with streaming desperation, to the shattered vessel itself. Then the storm began to abate and the wreck, driven hither and thither by winds, was heaved up on to a beach. Some half dozen sailors, the ship's captain and a solitary passenger gave thanks to God, and limped wearily ashore.

"What country, friends, is this?" asked the passenger, as the sun came out, and made the morning gold.

"This is Illyria, lady," answered the captain.

"And what should I do in Illyria?" she wept, gazing towards the dazzled sea. "My brother he is in Elysium." Her name was Viola and her brother had been called Sebastian; but now, surely, he was drowned. They had been twins, alike as two mornings in April, full of young beauty and promise. The kindly captain tried to reassure her that her brother might still live, for he had been seen, clinging to a spar; and Viola was glad enough to clutch at this frail straw even as her brother had clutched at his.

"Knowest thou this country?" she asked. The Captain knew it well, and told her of the Duke and his love for Olivia, and of how matters stood between them. Viola sighed; dearly she would have liked to

2

serve the lady, who mourned a brother even as she did herself. But it was not to be, as the lady would admit none to her house, so Viola begged the captain to bring her to the court of Duke Orsino where, in man's clothing, she might get employment as a page.

She called herself Cesario, and, in doublet and hose, with sword at her hip, and plumed hat in her hand, she made as handsome a youth as she had been beautiful as a girl. Gladly the Duke took her into his service; and, so much trust did he place in her that, after only three days, he sent her to the lady Olivia to plead his love. "Be not denied access," he urged her. "Stand at her doors."

"I'll do my best," promised Viola, and set off to bear her master's heart to the lady's house. It was a bitter errand; for that which she carried she would sooner have kept for herself. In the space of the three days, she had fallen in love with the Duke.

Olivia was not well pleased when she was told that there was a young man waiting at her gate who would not be sent away. Nor was she better pleased when she learned that her uncle was with him. Shrewdly she judged that the sight, smell and sound of Sir Toby would give no very favourable impression of a house in mourning. So she sent her steward, Malvolio, to tell the young man to go away, and to contradict, in his solemn person, any wild notion the young man might have got from Sir Toby. Malvolio was as sober a personage as Sir Toby was not, with a face as long as Sunday, which he wore on every day of the week. Before his important tread, the very larder mice grew serious and thought of church; but not even he could dislodge Duke Orsino's messenger from Olivia's gate.

"Let him approach," said the lady, with weary resignation; and, when Malvolio had stalked away to

3

admit the young person, she bade Maria, her waiting-woman, to fetch her veil.

"The honourable lady of the house, which is she?" demanded Viola, coming into the chamber with a stride that was too long for her, a look that was too bold, and a voice that was too deep. Then, when she had been coldly informed which was the mistress and which was the maid, she begged the veiled one to grant an audience alone. Olivia considered the request. Although there was an impertinence in the messenger's manner, and he had, from all accounts, been impudent at her gate, there was such a manly boldness about him (bolder by far than his too-gentle master), that the lady was curious to know him better. She dismissed her maid and leaned forward so that her eyes sparkled like stars within the night of her veil.

"Good madam, let me see your face," begged Viola, stepping a little outside her office and yielding to womanly curiosity. Olivia hesitated and then, not wanting it to be thought that she wore a veil merely to hide a plain countenance, drew it back and smiled a most radiant smile.

"Is't not well done?" she asked, with quiet pride.

"Excellently done," granted Viola, none too pleased to see a beauty that almost rivalled her own, "if God did all."

"'Tis in grain, sir," returned the lady, a little taken aback that the honesty of her complexion should be called into question. "'Twill endure wind and weather."

Viola, anxious to make amends for her offence, and fearful, perhaps, that its very shrewdness might have betrayed her for a woman, began pleading the Duke's cause with such passion and ardour, with such tender fire and aching love, as any woman might have dreamed of hearing from a lover's lips, but never did.

4

She spoke for the Duke as she longed for the Duke to have spoken to her.

"What is your parentage?" murmured Olivia faintly, when the messenger had done.

"Above my fortunes," answered Viola, somewhat surprised. "I am a gentleman."

Olivia sighed and nodded, and bade the messenger return to the Duke. "I cannot love him," she said. "Let him send no more . . ." She paused, and then added softly, "unless, perchance, you come to me again, to tell me how he takes it."

When the handsome youth had gone, Olivia gazed after him with brightly shining eyes. She summoned her steward. "Run after that same peevish messenger," she told him with a calmness that she herself marvelled at. "He left this ring behind him . . . tell him I'll none of it."

When her steward had gone with the ring, she blushed for her lie. The youth had left nothing; the ring had been her own. The messenger had pleaded the master's cause with too much success. The lady had fallen in love with the messenger, and longed for him to come again.

Malvolio, his black cloak flapping and his black stockings twinkling, like a crow to a feast, panted after the Duke's messenger. "Were not you even now, with the Countess Olivia?" he demanded when he had caught up with the youth; and, when the messenger had confessed as much, he said: "She returns this ring to you," and held out the trinket disdainfully, between finger and thumb.

Much surprised, Viola disclaimed all knowledge of the ring, so Malvolio dropped it contemptuously in the mire and hastened back to his mistress's house. Viola picked up the ring, stared at it, wondered, then guessed the reason for the sending of it. "Poor lady!" she sighed. Though the sun shone, the blossoms smiled and the air was soft, it was a sad world. She loved Orsino, who loved Olivia, who now, it seemed, loved her. In each instance, love was given, and not returned.

That night, in Olivia's house, there was another giver who got no return. Sir Andrew Aguecheek, still laying out his money for a cause that all but a fool would have known to be hopeless, was with his good friend, Sir Toby Belch. They were both drunk and inclined to be musical: Sir Toby low, and Sir Andrew high and eager as a wren. They sat at a table in a golden cave of candlelight, that, as they breathed, swayed and tottered as if the very air was tipsy from recollected wine. Presently they were joined by Feste, Olivia's jester, an ageing Fool who earned his keep by roaming the mansion and dispensing faded laughter and sad sweet songs. All three now leaned together in their withered finery, like a bowl of old mottled fruit.

"Would you have a love-song, or a song of good life?" proposed Feste.

"A love-song, a love-song!" belched Sir Toby, with an amorous glint in his wine-rich eye.

"Ay, ay," agreed Sir Andrew eagerly. "I care not for good life."

So Feste sang them a love-song of such sweet melancholy that they fell silent; and when he finished with: "Then come kiss me, sweet and twenty, Youth's a stuff will not endure," they sighed and their eyes grew moist; it was December remembering May. But melancholy was soon blown to the winds, for they began upon a mad song that went round and round, like a blindfold child at a birthday, which required much banging of tankards and stamping of feet to keep it in motion.

"What a caterwauling do you keep here!" Maria, a

6

cross plump morsel in her shift, had to shout to make herself heard, for the revellers had awakened the house. But she was too pretty a complainant to be taken seriously. Sir Toby staggered to his feet, caught her in his arms, and danced her about the room, singing at the top of his voice.

"For the love o' God, peace!" she shrieked, but more in laughter than reproach.

Then, when the uproar was at its height, with Feste capering, Sir Andrew whirling like a blown leaf, and the very plates upon the table jigging up and down, there appeared in the doorway a most fearful, dismal, chilling sight. Malvolio in his night-gown, with every inch of him, from tasselled cap to the shocked toes of his bare feet expressing outrage and indignation, stood and surveyed the lunatic scene. "My masters, are you mad?" he demanded; and then went on, in dreadful tones, to threaten Sir Toby, in his mistress's name, with eviction from the house unless he mended his ways.

"Dost thou think," returned Sir Toby indignantly, "because thou art virtuous, there shall be no more cakes and ale?"

Malvolio ignored him and, after having expressed strong disapproval of Maria, for being party to the drunken disorder, he stalked away like a ghost to the tomb.

"Go shake your ears!" said Maria angrily; and then, exasperated by the pompous steward, confided in Sir Toby a certain plan she had devised for humbling that odious man.

She would write a letter, in her mistress's hand, containing a passionate declaration of love for a person not named, but warmly described. She would drop this letter directly in Malvolio's way. Such was his vanity and high opinion of himself that, when he picked it up and read it, he would unfailingly see

7

himself as being the object of the Countess Olivia's love. The conspirators beamed happily at one another at the prospect of Malvolio's antics when he believed his mistress was his slave. While Sir Toby and his companions were plotting to make free with Olivia's love, Viola took back the refusal of it to Duke Orsino. Her feelings were mingled. She was a little saddened for the sadness Olivia's message caused her master, and thankful that it gave her hope of, one day, gaining Orsino for herself.

The Duke would hear none but the most doleful ditties, which chimed in with his mood. He bade his page go to the Countess Olivia once more to plead his love.

"But if she cannot love you, sir?" said Viola gently. But the Duke would take no such answer; so Viola, as nearly as she dared, tried to turn Orsino's thoughts towards herself. "My father had a daughter loved a man," she said, "as it might be, perhaps, were I a woman, I should your lordship."

The Duke gazed curiously at his page. "And what's her history?" he asked.

"A blank, my lord: she never told her love."

"But died thy sister of her love, my boy?" asked the Duke, when he had heard a sad tale of unspoken affection.

"I am all the daughters of my father's house," answered Viola, mysteriously; then grief swept over her as she thought of lost Sebastian. "And all the brothers too . . ." She turned away to hide the sorrow and the love she dared not show; and was thankful to escape Orsino's eye, even though her errand, to Olivia's house, was even less to her liking than before.

Now the Countess Olivia had a garden, where close-clipped trees made green secrets of the avenues and walks. Here Sir Toby and his companions had hid themselves and were peering eagerly through a lattice-work of branches, for Malvolio was coming, and the fateful letter lay directly in his way.

He came, a blot of ink upon the bright morning, with his shadow in close attendance, like an admiring pupil. He was in a gravely sauntering mood, with his buckled shoes making stately little patterns on the path. Sometimes he paused and bowed courteously to some imaginary acquaintance, sometimes he made gestures as if to indicate an audience with him was at an end. He was communing with himself aloud, as men will do when they suppose their only listeners are the trees. First, Maria was in love with him; and then, advancing further into dreams, he was Count Malvolio, had been married to Olivia for three months, was richly dressed and had just summoned his wife's uncle to stand before him as a penitent. "Cousin Toby," he murmured reproachfully, "you must amend your drunkenness."

"Out, scab!" breathed Sir Toby, trembling with rage at the steward's presumption. Then he and his fellow watchers held their breath. Malvolio had seen the letter. He touched it with his foot; looked cautiously about him; then picked the letter up and immediately recognized his mistress's hand! With shaking fingers he broke the seal and read:

"Jove knows I love: But who?" There followed some riddling lines that ended with: "M.O.A.I. doth sway my life."

He cogitated, long and deep; and then, with a burst of excitement, he realised that M.O.A.I. were all letters that were in his own name. He read on; and every word he read convinced him more and more that the letter was from his lady and was meant for him. "If this fall into thy hand," she wrote, "revolve. In my stars I am above thee, but be not afraid of greatness. Some are born great, some achieve great-

ness, and some have greatness thrust upon 'em."
Then she urged him to be haughty in his manner, for
was not his future golden? He should smile in her
presence to show that he returned her love; and she
earnestly requested him to appear in yellow stockings with cross garters.

The solemn steward was transfigured with joy. He
hopped, he danced, he kissed the letter and pressed it
to his breast. His dearest dreams had been fulfilled.
He would be his mistress's master, and lord of the
mansion. He kissed the letter again and, black and
flapping, capered away!

"Mark his first approach before my lady," promised
Maria, as the conspirators came out of their hiding-
place, weeping with laughter. "He will come to her in
yellow stockings, and 'tis a colour she abhors, and
cross-gartered, a fashion she detests."

Viola, on her way to perform her master's errand,
came striding through the garden; but before she
could enter the mansion, Olivia herself, in mourning
more gorgeous than ever, came out, together with
Maria.

"Most excellent, accomplished lady," exclaimed
Viola, doffing her great plumed hat and bowing low,
"the heavens rain odours on you!"

Sir Toby and Sir Andrew, who were eagerly awaiting the appearance of Malvolio, looked askance at
the Duke's extravagant page.

"That youth's a rare courtier," muttered Sir
Andrew, enviously, "'rain odours' – well!" And even
when the Countess made it plain that she wished to
hear the Duke's message alone, he lingered,
unnecessary as a maypole in June. At length, he was
persuaded to follow his companions; and Olivia, sinking down upon a rustic bench, gazed warmly at the
page.

"Give me your hand," she commanded gently.

With the utmost reluctance Viola surrendered her hand, and took it back as soon as she could, for Olivia showed every sign of pressing it to her bosom. She tried to plead her master's cause, and to avert her eyes from Olivia's ardent eyes and heaving breast. She tried to back away, but Olivia, with a silken rustle that was, in Viola's ears, more terrible than the pursuing of a tiger, followed after. "Dear lady – " pleaded Viola; but Olivia, overcome with passion, abandoned all restraint, and poured out her love for the Duke's handsome, retreating page. The more she was refused, the greater grew her desire, for it was like any other hunger that increases with denial.

"And so adieu, good madam," cried Viola, when, by a mixture of ingenious avoiding and desperate cunning, she had got herself to the gate.

"Yet come again," begged Olivia, as the youth escaped.

Sir Andrew, whose amorous hopes had been kept alight by Sir Toby, was in despair. "I saw your niece," he said to his fat comforter, "do more favours to the Count's serving-man than ever she bestowed upon me." He was all for giving up his courtship of Olivia, but Sir Toby, anxious not to lose so easy a supply of money, persuaded him otherwise. He put it to Sir Andrew that Olivia, by showing favour to the page, had meant only to stir up Sir Andrew to valour. He advised Sir Andrew to challenge the youth to a duel. Sir Andrew nodded, and, when he had gone to write out the challenge, Sir Toby reflected that no great harm would come out of the encounter; for Sir Andrew and the youth were about as fierce and warlike as each other. Then Maria, shaking with laughter, came to warn him that Malvolio, in yellow

11

stockings and cross-gartered, and full of bedroom smirks and bony smiles, was coming to the Countess.

Poor Olivia! she was as mistakenly loved as she was mistakenly in love. Unable to bear his absence any longer, she sent a servant after Orsino's page, to plead with him to return.

Now as Viola was returning to the palace of the Duke, another Viola was in the town: same height, same face, same hat, same doublet and same boots. Yet not quite the same. It was Sebastian. He had not been drowned. He had been washed ashore, where, mourning his lost sister (who was, to him, as lost as he to her), he had been discovered by a gentleman by the name of Antonio. Antonio had helped him and never left his side; and now they walked together in the town.

"What's to do?" asked Sebastian, gazing with interest round the busy streets. "Shall we go see the reliques of this town?"

But Antonio would not; he had, in the past, fought against the Duke, and was still counted as an enemy. Nonetheless he urged Sebastian to walk about and view the noble buildings of the town. "Here's my purse," he said, for he knew Sebastian had no money and might see something he wished to buy. He had grown deeply fond of the youth, and thought nothing of trusting him with all his wealth. Gratefully Sebastian took his friend's purse, and promised to meet with him at a certain inn, within an hour. They parted, Sebastian one way, and Antonio another; but it was not long before Antonio, finding he needed money for his lodgings, was forced to go in search of Sebastian to ask for the return of his purse.

Olivia, gazing out of her window for the hoped-for return of Orsino's page, was sadder than her black;

for the scorn of one loved was more painful by far than a brother's decease. "Where's Malvolio?" she asked. "He is sad and civil, and suits well for a servant with my fortunes."

"He is coming, madam," said Maria, "but in very strange manner."

The solemn steward had obeyed the letter to the very letter: his cross-gartered legs were as yellow as primroses, and he smiled.

"How now, Malvolio?" exclaimed Olivia, not a little surprised.

"Sweet Lady, ho, ho!" ventured Malvolio, persevering with his smile, even though his legs were painful as his garters were too tight. He winked at the Countess, kissed his fingers at her, and smirked with all his teeth.

Maria turned away; her shoulders were shaking with inward laughter.

"Why, how dost thou, man?" demanded Olivia, angrily. "What is the matter with thee?"

Malvolio, with a saucy twinkle of his feet (which gave him some discomfort and caused him to rub his constricted legs), made answer with an obscure reference to the letter he had received. The Countess, not understanding, became worried about him. "Wilt thou go to bed, Malvolio?" she suggested kindly.

"To bed?" cried Malvolio, ambition leaping within him. "Ay, sweetheart, and I'll come to thee!"

He held out his arms, but, for one reason or another, the Countess did not fly into his embrace. He pursued the matter, with further references to the letter, but before he could get his mistress to confess her love, they were interrupted with the news that the Duke's messenger had returned and was awaiting the Countess's pleasure.

"I'll come to him," said Olivia quickly; and bade

Maria to fetch Sir Toby to look after her poor steward, who, she felt, had lost his wits.

Malvolio, alone, was not displeased with the way things had gone. Everything the Countess had said, fitted, or could be made to fit, with his high expectations. The very fact that she had asked for her kinsman, Sir Toby, to attend him, proved that she held him in the highest regard.

Sir Toby came, and Malvolio was condescending with him. After all, he would soon be master of the house. Then, Sir Toby and his drunken companions would be put in their proper place. "Go hang yourselves all," he said contemptuously, to his mistress's uncle, her maid, and a servant by the name of Fabian, for whom he had a particular dislike. "You are idle, shallow things; I am not of your element. You shall know more hereafter."

"Come, we'll have him in a dark room and bound," said Sir Toby when the steward had limped and stalked away. Now that the Countess thought that Malvolio was mad, he should be treated as such. He had aspired to love, and was not love madness?

Viola's audience with Olivia had been brief. Again the Countess had begged for love; and again it had been refused. "Well, come again tomorrow," had pleaded the distracted lady. Viola sighed, and left, only to be accosted at the mansion's gate by the lady's portly uncle and a servant whose looks were grave.

"Gentleman, God save thee," said Sir Toby, with much solemnity. Sir Andrew's challenge to the page had been written so foolishly that it would have provoked more laughter than fear, so Sir Toby had decided to deliver the challenge by word of mouth. Quietly he advised the page to look to his defence, for he had offended a very dangerous person.

"You mistake, sir," stammered Viola, growing pale. "I am sure no man hath any quarrel to me."

"You'll find it otherwise, I assure you," said Sir Toby grimly; and went on to present so fearsome a picture of the person who desired satisfaction, that Viola shook with terror.

"I will return again into the house," cried Viola, preferring by far to face a love-sick woman than an angry man, "and desire some conduct of the lady." But it was not to be; and Sir Toby, leaving the trembling Viola in the charge of Fabian, went to fetch her deadly adversary, Sir Andrew Aguecheek.

"Why, man, he is a very devil," confided Sir Toby to Sir Andrew, when he had found him.

"Pox on't," cried Sir Andrew, turning paler than his linen. "I'll not meddle with him."

"Ay," agreed Sir Toby, "but he will not now be pacified: Fabian can scarce hold him yonder."

This was very true, as Fabian was having the utmost difficulty in keeping Viola from bolting for her life.

"There's no remedy, sir," called out Sir Toby, coming out of the mansion and dragging Sir Andrew after him. "He will fight with you for's oath's sake!"

"Pray God defend me!" wailed Viola, struggling in the grip of Fabian, even as Sir Andrew tugged at Sir Toby's. "A little thing would make me tell them how much I lack of a man."

But the seconds were restless, and the two shaking heroes were propelled towards one another on feet that scarcely touched the ground.

"I do assure you, 'tis against my will!" sobbed Viola, as if Sir Andrew might have supposed it to be otherwise; and drew her sword.

Sir Andrew, with no more enthusiasm, drew his; and there they stood, propped up by their seconds, with their blades waving, like grass in the wind.

15

"Put up your sword! If this young gentleman have done offence, I take the fault on me!"

A gentleman, passing by the mansion's gate, had seen the imminent battle and had drawn his own sword to halt it. It was Antonio. He had been searching for Sebastian and now believed that he had found him, and in danger of his life. But before more could be done, a party of the Duke's officers came by. At once, Antonio was recognized and arrested as the Duke's enemy.

"This comes with seeking you," said Antonio, somewhat bitterly to Viola, and asked for the return of his purse. "I must entreat of you some of that money," repeated Antonio, as Viola showed no sign of understanding him.

"What money, sir?" wondered Viola.

"Will you deny me now?" demanded Antonio, amazed that the youth he had befriended should prove to be so shameless a villain. He reminded the youth of the kindnesses he had done him.

"I know of none," protested Viola, her confusion increasing.

"O Heavens themselves!" cried out Antonio, more distressed by the youth's ingratitude than by the officers who held him by the arms.

"Come sir, I pray you go," commanded one of his captors; but before they dragged him away, Antonio declared to all how much he had done for the youth, and how little he was getting in recompense. He told of how he had saved him from death, how he had comforted him and supported him, and of how he had come to love him.

"What's that to us?" grunted an officer. "The time goes by. Away!"

"O how vile an idol proves this god!" shouted Antonio, pointing at Viola as he was borne away. "Thou hast, Sebastian, done good feature shame!"

Then he was gone, leaving behind him Sir Toby and Sir Andrew with a very poor opinion of Viola, who they supposed to be, not only a cowardly, but a monstrously ungrateful youth; and Viola with a tempest of feelings in her breast.

"He named Sebastian!" she breathed. Antonio had taken her for her brother; therefore Sebastian was alive! She fled back to the Duke.

If the mistake of one face for another had caused a man to despair, it soon brought a woman to rejoice. Sebastian, wandering past the Countess's mansion, was instantly accosted by Sir Toby and Sir Andrew.

"Now, sir, have I met you again?" cried Sir Andrew, made bold by all he had seen of the youth's courage. "There's for you!" And he struck him in the face.

"Why, there's for thee, and there, and there!" cried Sebastian, angrily returning Sir Andrew's blow, and with such interest as sent the knight reeling to the ground. Sir Toby drew his sword; Sebastian drew his, and blood would surely have been shed, had not the Countess herself come out to discover the cause of the commotion at her gate. Angrily she dismissed Sir Toby, and begged the young man's pardon for the antics of her drunken uncle, who aggravated her beyond measure. Then with such speaking looks and deep-felt sighs, that made her meaning as plain as she herself was lovely, begged the young man come within. Sebastian blinked. "If it be thus to dream," he marvelled, "still let me sleep!" And, unwilling to let slip what Providence had provided, followed Olivia into her house.

Sebastian, finding himself to be beloved for no reason he could think of, walked in brightness; but Malvolio, who believed himself to be loved for reasons of his own worth, was plunged into gloom. He had paid the penalty for greatness; he had risen high, and had fallen low.

Sir Toby and his companions had got their revenge. They had declared Malvolio to be mad; for what could be madder than for a steward to suppose his noble mistress was in love with him? They had locked him away in a dark chamber from which he cried out piteously to be released.

"Sir Topas," he wailed, to Feste, Olivia's jester, who had dressed himself as a curate to torment the steward to the very limits of endurance, "never was man thus wronged! Do not think I am mad. They have laid me here in hideous darkness – "

But his captors were unrelenting. It had not been enough for Malvolio to be ridiculous in the world's eyes, he had to be humbled in his own. For as long as he thought himself to be great, the world's opinion counted for little. But at length Sir Toby yielded, not to the promptings of pity, for he had none, but because he feared that his niece would lose all patience with him if he continued to abuse her solemn steward. The wretched man was allowed to write a letter to his mistress, pleading to be released.

Even as a false priest had conducted Malvolio to hell, so a true one brought Olivia to heaven. Before the young man, whom she still took to be Cesario, the Duke's page, could change his mind and run away, she took him firmly to a chapel in the town where a holy father married them without delay. Sebastian submitted gladly for, although he guessed that he was loved by mistake, he felt it would be folly to set the lady right. He loved her. Then, the wedding done, he left his bride of minutes to find Antonio and give him back his purse.

It was late afternoon. The sun had painted certain windows red and gold, and laid dark carpets along the streets. The Duke and his lords, and Viola, came strolling through the town, where they met Olivia's jester. At once the Duke paid Feste well to go and fetch his mistress for, in spite of all Olivia's refusals, Orsino had not given up hope of winning her.

Feste departed and then came calamities, so swiftly one upon another that there was scarcely reeling time between them! First Antonio, in the grip of officers and on his way to gaol, came marching by.

"Here comes the man, sir, that did rescue me," said Viola, recognizing her saviour from the duel. The Duke also recognized him, not as a saviour but as a very warlike enemy. He accused him; Viola defended him. Antonio turned upon Viola and accused her yet again of base ingratitude; and again Viola denied it.

"Here comes the Countess," cried the Duke, forgetting enemies and friends alike, as the object of his heart approached. "Gracious Olivia – "

But she would have none of him and had eyes only for his page.

"Where goes Cesario?" she cried, when, as Orsino turned to leave, Viola prepared to follow.

"After him I love . . ." returned Viola; and Olivia's worst fears were realised. The young man had changed his mind.

"Hast thou forgot thyself? Is it so long?" she demanded. "Call forth the holy father!" And then, when her pleas had no effect, she begged: "Cesario, husband, stay!"

"Husband?" exclaimed the Duke, amazed.

"Ay, husband."

"Her husband, sirrah?"

"No, my lord, not I!" swore Viola, as the Duke turned upon her in a rage.

But proof was at hand. The holy father came in answer to Olivia's summons, and confirmed that he had only just married the lady and the youth.

19

"O thou dissembling cub!" cried out the Duke, in anguish that his page, whom he had loved and trusted, should have so betrayed him.

"My lord, I do protest – " pleaded Viola; but before matters could be explained, yet another blow fell and added to the dreadful confusion. Sir Andrew Aguecheek, bleeding from his least useful part, which was his head, came staggering down the street, calling for a surgeon.

"Who has done this, Sir Andrew?" asked the Countess.

"The Count's gentleman, one Cesario," groaned Sir Andrew, clutching his wound. "We took him for a coward, but he's the very devil incardinate." Then he saw Viola and shrank back in terror. Next came Sir Toby, leaning on the jester's arm. He too was bleeding from a wound that was the very twin of Sir Andrew's, and which had been given him by the same fierce Cesario.

"Get him to bed," commanded the Countess, concerned for her uncle, "and let his hurt be looked to."

With moans and groans and angry belches, Sir Toby and Sir Andrew were helped away, leaving pale Viola condemned by all for an almanack of crimes: by the Duke for treachery, by Antonio for ingratitude, by Olivia for faithlessness, and by Sir Toby and Sir Andrew for assault. She trembled; she turned from one accuser to another. What could she say? To deny treachery made her seem more treacherous; to deny ingratitude made her seem the more ungrateful; to deny faithlessness made her seem stony-hearted; and to deny assault made her a bare-faced liar when the wounds had been seen by all. Nothing less than a miracle could have absolved her, at a single stroke, from so many crimes.

"I am sorry, madam, I have hurt your kinsman,"

said another Cesario, stepping forward like a reflection without a glass.

"One face, one voice, one habit, and two persons!" whispered Orsino, staring from one Cesario to the other.

"How have you made division of yourself?" wondered Antonio.

"Most wonderful!" sighed Olivia, when she had determined which was her husband and which was not.

Then brother and sister embraced one another and wept with joy.

"Boy," said the Duke to his page, when at last Sebastian and Viola stood apart, "thou hast said to me a thousand times thou never shouldst love woman like to me." The sight of so much fondness had swelled his tender heart, and the untangling of so much distress into so much love had made him long to have a part in it. "Give me thy hand," he said to Viola, "and let me see thee in thy woman's weeds." She gave him her hand and he pressed it to his lips. Suddenly he loved her, for he knew that she loved him; and there's nothing so awakens love as love itself.

Only Malvolio still languished in darkness. The letter he had written was brought to Olivia, who, when she read it, took pity on the poor man and commanded his immediate release. He came, crumpled and dishevelled, with straw in his hair, for the chamber in which he had been locked was none of the cleanest. Bitterly he accused his mistress of having misled him, and showed her the letter that had set his madness on. She took the paper and studied it. She shook her head: the hand was not hers. "Alas, poor fool, how have they baffled thee!" she said, with a gentle shake of her head when she had divined who had been the authors of Malvolio's fall.

The steward glared about him. The general happiness of pairs and pairings warmed him into no better utterance than: "I'll be revenged on the whole pack of you!" Then he stalked away.

But Malvolio's departure cast no gloom on the company; for his injuries had been to his pride and not to his heart; and so were not fatal.

Then Viola, who had gained the love of Orsino and hung upon his arm, and Olivia, who had gained the love of Sebastian, and hung upon his arm, and Antonio who had regained his purse and his faith in the gratitude of friends, and all at a single stroke, strolled away in a golden pattern of plaited arms and inclining heads.

Feste alone remained behind. He gazed after the happy ones, and, seating himself cross-legged on the ground, sang one of his sweet sad songs:

"When that I was and a little tiny boy,
    With hey, ho, the wind and the rain,
A foolish thing was but a toy,
    For the rain it raineth every day."

Though he was my lady's Fool, he was the wisest of all. He was paid to play the Fool; the rest of the world did it for nothing.

The Tempest

Far, far away, upon the shore of a strange island that was forever wrapped in mists that the sun changed into moving curtains of gold, there sat an ageing man and his young, lovely daughter. They were staring out to sea. About the man's shoulders was a blue cloak, embroidered all over with silver, and beside him on the sands lay a carved staff and a book as thick and richly bound as a Bible. Sometimes his hand rested on the book, and sometimes upon his daughter's arm, as if to comfort her. His face was calm; hers was pale and frightened.

They were watching a ship that was about to be smashed into pieces. A tempest had seized it, an uncanny fury of the elements that seemed to enclose it in a swirling black bubble. As it heaved and tossed, its masts scribbled frantic messages against the blotchy sky, and its rigging all fell down like a madman's hair. Tiny figures, black as fleas, and with patched white faces, clung where they could; and shrieks and screams, small as the squealing of mice, drifted to the watchers on the shore. Then it was over. Fire, liquid as blazing ink, ran along the yards. The timbers snarled and cracked, the ship split, and was lost. The tempest subsided, the dark bubble dispersed, and the sea was calm.

"Be collected," comforted the father, his arm about his daughter's trembling shoulders: "no more amazement: tell your piteous heart there's no harm done."

He spoke the truth. He himself, Prospero the enchanter, had raised the storm and, as he promised his daughter Miranda, not a soul had been lost. He had, by his strange power, brought them all safe to the island.

He stood up, and, frowning, began to pace to and fro, making little yellow tempests in the sand, which his long, heavy cloak smoothed away, so that he seemed to have walked, invisibly, on air. Silently Miranda watched . . .

Presently he halted. He smiled at her inquiring looks and then, putting off his cloak, that mysteriously glittering garment into which had been woven, by his own deep skill, all his magical powers, he seated himself beside her. At last the time had come for him to tell her how they had come to this strange isle, what they had been before, and why he had raised the tempest that had wrecked the ship.

"Canst thou remember a time before we came?" he asked, but more as master to pupil than father to child. She faltered upon some dim recollection of shadowy serving women. He brushed it aside, and then began to tell her a tale of such grim happenings that his eyes burned with anger at the memory of them, even though they had taken place far away and long ago.

She had indeed had serving women, and many of them, for she was the only child of a Duke. He, Prospero, her humble, solitary father, had once been a rich and mighty prince; the Duke of Milan, no less. But he had been such a ruler that the outward show of greatness and the exercise of princely power had mattered less to him than the kingdom of the mind. "My library," he confided to Miranda, "was dukedom large enough . . ." So, to free himself for the study that he loved, he had given over the tediousness of government to one he had trusted with all his heart: his brother Antonio.

But alas! he had been more wise in books than in hearts, and as he uttered his brother's name, his brow darkened and Miranda grew frightened as, for the first time, the chill of human wickedness touched her bright world.

Antonio, not content with the use of power, wanted the reality and the semblance of it, too. In exchange for the promise of the dukedom, he conspired with the King of Naples, sworn enemy of Milan; and, one night, he opened the city's gates and let the enemy in. Milan fell, and Duke Prospero was overthrown.

"Wherefore did they not that hour destroy us?" asked Miranda, for her father's brother seemed limitless in his evil.

Prospero shook his head. He and his infant daughter had not been spared out of pity, but because Antonio had feared the consequence of public crime. Instead, he had cast them adrift, in a rotting craft, with neither mast nor sail, and trusted in the blind elements to do his murders secretly. And so it would have happened, had not a kindly Neapolitan, by name of Gonzalo, furnished them with food and drink, with clothing and with those precious volumes from Prospero's library from which the enchanter had learned his power.

Long, long they had drifted, the father and his crying child, until at last they had come to this uncanny isle, where, for twelve years now, they had lived together with none but each other for human company.

"And now, I pray you, sir," murmured Miranda, her mind heavy with bewilderment, "your reason for raising this sea-storm?"

Prospero's eyes gleamed with triumph. The vessel had contained his enemies. Now they were all ashore

25

and within his grasp. "Here cease more questions," he commanded. "Thou art inclined to sleep . . ." He laid a hand on her head. She smiled and sighed, and closed her eyes; and, in a moment, was asleep. Gently Prospero smoothed her golden hair and brushed away the sand that might have troubled her face.

He stood up and put on his cloak once more. He looked up at the sky, then to the sea, then to the island's haunted woods. "Come away, servant, come," he called softly. "I am ready now. Approach, my Ariel, come."

There was a thin noise, as of wind across lute strings, and with a flash and a whirl and a quick unwinding of air, Prospero's servant appeared.

An odd servant: a slight, weird, dancing, darting servant, very bright to look at, never still save for trembling dragonfly moments, forever trying on faces, as if at the tailor's . . .

"All hail, great master! Grave sir, hail!" cried Ariel, with a thousand courtly bows, all performed in the twinkling of an eye.

"Hast thou, spirit," asked the enchanter, "performed to point the tempest that I bade thee?"

"To every article," promised the spirit, with another bright parcel of bows; and told, with eager and child-like delight, of the frantic terror aboard the ship, of how the passengers had flung themselves, shrieking, into the sea, and Ferdinand, the King of Naples' son, had cried out: "Hell is empty, and all the devils are here!"

Prospero smiled and Ariel, encouraged by such a mark of approval, went on to tell how all had been brought ashore, miraculously fresh and dry, as if the tempest had never been. They had been dispersed in groups about the island, none knowing of any other's having survived. Even the vessel itself had been restored in every particular and now lay in a harbour with the sailors safely under hatches and locked fast in a dreamless sleep.

"The King's son have I landed by himself," said Ariel, with a queer, sideways smile . . .

Prospero nodded, and then proposed still more work for his servant; between now and nightfall, much needed to be done. But Ariel scowled.

"How now, moody?" demanded Prospero, angered by the spirit's peevish looks. "What is't thou canst demand?"

"My liberty."

But Ariel's service still had two days more to run; and Prospero, frowning at the spirit's presumption, so that Ariel shrank before him, reminded his servant of how that servitude had first begun. Had Ariel forgotten how things were when Prospero and Miranda had first come to the isle?

Ariel had not; nonetheless, despite wild shakings of the head and imploring looks, Prospero reminded the spirit that the isle had been filled, not with airy music, but with desolate howls and moans that proceeded from deep in a cleft in a pine tree. There Ariel had been imprisoned by Sycorax, a foul witch, for refusing to obey her worst commands. Sycorax had died, leaving her misshapen son, Caliban, to rule the isle, and Ariel in hopeless wailing misery.

From this misery Prospero had freed the spirit, and, in return, had demanded twelve years of absolute obedience.

"If thou more murmur'st," threatened Prospero, "I will rend an oak and peg thee in his knotty entrails . . ."

At once the frightened spirit was all willingness to obey and do anything to please the great enchanter.

"Do so," said Prospero; "and after two days I will discharge thee."

"That's my noble master! What shall I do? Say what; what shall I do?"

Prospero smiled at his servant's anxiety and then bade Ariel take on the shape of a sea-nymph, and to be visible to none but himself. Once more there was a noise as of wind across lute strings, and Ariel was gone.

The enchanter gazed after his servant with a deep fondness. Not for more worlds than Ariel could have given him would he have punished that wayward spirit. He bent down and awakened his still sleeping daughter.

"Come on," he proposed, as she rubbed her eyes and smiled at him; "we'll visit Caliban, my slave."

"'Tis a villain, sir," protested Miranda. Prospero shook his head. Even villains had their uses, and Caliban's was to fetch wood and do all manner of menial toil.

"Caliban!" he called, as they approached a dwelling made of rough stones and rock. "Thou earth, thou! speak!"

"There's wood enough within," came a voice as thick and harsh as tangled briers; but before Prospero could command again, a fragile sea-nymph, with Ariel's eager eyes, and Ariel's bows and dartings, whirled to his side, hovered, took softly breathed instruction, and sped away upon a mysterious errand. Then Prospero turned back to his other servant on the isle. "Thou poisonous slave!" he shouted. "Come forth!" and Caliban, unable to defy his great master any longer, came cursing out of his hovel.

A slow, heavy, lumbering creature, all scowls and bristles, with his ugly nakedness scarcely covered by skins as rough and hairy as his own; a creature of darkness, like the foul witch who had borne him, and of curses, like the devil who had fathered him.

"This island's mine, by Sycorax my mother," he

28

snarled, but crouching low before the enchanter whom he feared even more than he hated. For Prospero had the power to fill him from top to toe with a thousand aches and dazzling pains that made him roar out in the night.

But it had not always been so, Caliban remembered. When Prospero had first come to the isle he had soothed and comforted Caliban, and taught him many marvellous things, so that Caliban had shown him all the secrets and wonders of the isle. It was then that Prospero had turned against him and had seized the island for himself . . .

"Thou most lying slave!" cried Prospero, pale with anger. His kindness to the misshapen creature that crouched, hatefully, at his feet, had only ceased when that creature, filled with lust, had sought to violate Miranda.

Caliban's sunken eyes gleamed at the memory. He turned his heavy head towards Miranda. She drew back in horror. "I pitied thee," she said, with bitter regret, "took pains to make thee speak . . ."

"You taught me language," answered Caliban, savagely, "and my profit on't is, I know how to curse!"

But because it had been gentle Miranda who had taught him to use the words, his very curses were musical; and because he knew no other way, helplessly he clothed the darkest and most brutish thoughts in the language of light.

"Hag-seed, hence!" commanded Prospero abruptly and, under threat of sharp aches and bone-grinding cramps, despatched the monster of the isle to fetch more fuel, for he had heard faint music in the air.

The sea-nymph returned, and with a strange catch from the sea. Playing upon a small, delicate stringed instrument, and singing very high and silvery, the spirit drew along, as if by invisible cords, a youth, richly dressed and noble in appearance.

"Come unto these yellow sands . . ." tempted the invisible Ariel; and the youth stumbled after, haunted and tantalized by the music in the air. It was Ferdinand, the King of Naples' son. He had been mourning the father he believed drowned, when he had heard the music and had followed it helplessly. For a moment the singing ceased, and the youth looked about him in bewilderment; then it began again:

> "Full fathom five thy father lies;
> Of his bones are coral made,
> Those are pearls that were his eyes . . ."

He sank down in despair as the song remembered his loss.

"Say what thou seest . . ." murmured Prospero to Miranda, for the youth was too wrapped in grief and the mysteries of the isle to see the watching enchanter and his daughter.

"What is't? a spirit?" breathed Miranda, lost in wonderment, for she had never seen a young man before.

"No, wench," smiled her father; "it eats and sleeps and hath such senses as we have."

Then Ferdinand saw Miranda.

"At the first sight they have changed eyes," breathed Prospero. "Delicate Ariel, I'll set thee free for this." Fondly he looked on as the youth and his daughter stood in amazed admiration of one another. Though Ferdinand, unlike the girl, was no stranger to his own kind, he had never seen such a one as she. Surely the magic of the isle had made its masterpiece, and whatever wonders were to come, none could outdazzle Miranda! Eagerly he explained that he was now the King of Naples as he feared his father had

30

perished in the storm; and, in a wild burst of adoration, offered to make Miranda the Queen.

Here Prospero intervened, and stepped between his daughter and the youth, cutting off the ardour of their looks. Their love had been so quick and sudden that he feared it could not last. Some testing time, some hardship, some obstacle to be overcome was needed to judge its strength.

Sternly he confronted Ferdinand. He was lying. He was not the King of Naples. He was a spy, set upon the island to seize it.

"No, as I am a man!" protested Ferdinand, peering from side to side round the grim father for a sight of his entrancing daughter; and Miranda, her head wandering likewise, like a waving flower, strongly supported him.

"Speak not you for him!" Prospero commanded, spreading his mantle to obscure her view. "He's a traitor. Come; I'll manacle thy neck and feet together . . ."

Angrily Ferdinand drew his sword. A foolish move. Prospero raised his staff, and Ferdinand felt the air turn to iron and fix him from head to toe.

"Beseech you, father!" implored Miranda, on behalf of the marble Ferdinand.

"Silence!" commanded Prospero, turning upon his daughter. What did she know of the world of men? "Having seen but him and Caliban," he said contemptuously. "Foolish wench! To the most of men this is a Caliban, and they to him are angels!"

"My affections are then most humble," cried Miranda, still striving, round her father, for another glimpse of Ferdinand; "I have no ambition to see a goodlier man!"

And Ferdinand too, released enough from enchantment to speak, pleaded his love. Let great Prospero chain and enslave him, he would willingly endure all, if, but once a day, even through prison bars, he might see Miranda.

Prospero, hiding his smiles, withdrew and, briefly, let their craning looks meet. Rapidly he murmured more instructions to the invisibly hovering Ariel, who nodded, bowed half a hundred times, and sped away. Then, resuming his sternness, he returned. "Come, follow!" he commanded Ferdinand harshly; and then to Miranda, who begged, pleaded and clung obstinately to his mantle, "Speak not for him!"

Though he was a mighty enchanter, with power over lightning, thunder, wind and rain, though he could turn men to stone, fill them with pains, and drowse them to sleep, though he could call up visions and bewitch the air, he had no power over love. There his authority stopped. All he could do was, by harsh pretence, to test the strength of it.

In another part of the island, in a green glade thickly curtained with trees, there was heaped up the richest treasure of the wrecked ship. A gathering of gorgeous castaways, velvet gentlemen, embroidered all over with crowns and coronets sat and strolled and debated their situation. Alonzo, the King of Naples, sat on the stump of a tree, his tragic head in his tragic hands, and mourned the loss of his son.

"Beseech you, sir, be merry," comforted an old councillor, by name of Gonzalo, and pointed out that the King had much to be thankful for. After all, he and his companions were saved and on dry land . . .

"Prithee, peace," said the King, in no mood for philosophy.

"He receives comfort like cold porridge," remarked the King's brother Sebastian, to Antonio, the Duke of Milan. They were a sharp, knowing, ambitious pair of gentlemen, men of the real world. Though they were pleased enough to find themselves alive, they were none too pleased to find themselves on such an island, far from courts and affairs. Nor were they better pleased with their company. The King was feeble and Gonzalo was a tedious old fool, fit for nothing but to laugh at.

"Here is everything advantageous to life," said Gonzalo, examining the grass, fingering the soil and peering at the trees through spectacles that enlarged all virtues to his kindly eyes.

"True," said Antonio mockingly; "save means to live."

They would not let him be. Whatever he praised, from the miracle of their salvation to the wonder of their clothing seeming fresh and new, they jeered at. Until, at last, the old man gave up.

"You are gentlemen of brave mettle," he said wearily. He yawned. Suddenly he was overcome by a strong desire for sleep. It was strange: there seemed to be a sound of music in the air, very sweet and heavy. And stranger still, some heard it and some did not. Of those who heard it, first Gonzalo, then two other lords, and then the grieving King himself, were overcome by its drowsy charm, and closed their eyes in sleep. Then the music ceased, and Ariel, the unseen musician, silently left the glade. The two who had heard nothing, remained awake, wide awake.

"What a strange drowsiness possesses them," wondered Sebastian, gazing round at the figures on the grass, who lay, quiet as painted people.

"It is the quality o' the climate," murmured Antonio, his eyes fixed upon the sleeping King. The two gentlemen stared at one another; and each saw in the other an image of himself. Each was brother to greatness; one had taken his chance and succeeded; the other's was still to come.

Antonio, still staring at the sleeping King, began to say something, as if to himself, then stopped, then sighed, then looked Sebastian quickly in the face, and murmured: "My strong imagination sees a crown dropping upon thy head."

Sebastian looked puzzled, and pretended not to catch the drift of Antonio's remark; but very quietly. It would be foolish to wake the sleepers. The two gentlemen began to stroll about, on tiptoe, and to peer and stare among the trees.

"Will you grant with me," proposed Antonio, reassuring himself that a shadow was not a watcher, "that Ferdinand is drowned?"

"He's gone," agreed Sebastian, confirming that a bush was not a spy.

"Then tell me," pursued Antonio, approaching the breathing King, "who's the next heir of Naples?"

The King's daughter. But she was Queen of Tunis, pointed out Antonio, and that was far from Naples. Carefully he measured with his eyes the distance between the helpless King and the helpless Gonzalo. Then he looked hard at Sebastian. Being damned himself in the destruction of a brother, he wanted company in his damnation. Sebastian nodded, and Antonio knew that the idea he had put into Sebastian's head had found a ready kennel.

"Draw thy sword," whispered Sebastian, nodding towards his sleeping brother.

"Draw together," breathed Antonio, not wanting to be the only murderer and so in another's power. He nodded towards Gonzalo. Then he drew his sword, but not until he had seen Sebastian do the same. Together they stood, poised for double murder.

Suddenly Gonzalo awoke! "Now good angels," he cried out, "preserve the King!" As if in a dream he had heard a high, silvery voice singing in his ear: "Shake off slumber and beware! Awake, awake!"

In a moment, all were awake and on their feet, and

34

staring with amazement at the two who stood, with glaring eyes and dangerous swords.

"Why are you drawn?" demanded the King, his hand upon his own weapon.

Confusedly, first Sebastian and then Antonio, said they had heard the roaring of lions nearby.

"Heard you this, Gonzalo?" asked the King. The old man frowned and admitted that he had indeed heard a strange sound that had awakened him. The King was satisfied; nonetheless, they must all leave the glade and continue the search, even though it was hopeless, for his lost son.

Mouse-eyed Ariel watched them go. There was nothing on the isle that could be unknown to the lord of it. Prospero, through the eyes of his servant, watched over all.

There was a growling of thunder and the sky was overcast. On a desolate part of the shore, where a leaden sea lapped upon leaden sands, Caliban toiled under his burden of wood. Savagely he cursed his master, who, for the smallest offence, visited him with biting terrors and with hissing snakes.

"Lo, now lo!" he cried out suddenly. "Here comes a spirit of his, and to torment me for bringing wood in slowly! I'll fall flat . . ."

And down the monster fell, flinging his stinking cloak over his stinking head, and leaving nothing visible but his hairy legs and feet.

The spirit approached; a queer spirit in patched colours with tiny bells sewn to points on his sleeves and cap, so that he jingled like a town of distant churches. It was Trinculo, the King of Naples' jester, an ageing fool who lived only on the echo of old jokes. Saved from the shipwreck by a Providence that plainly did not know right from wrong, he wandered across the shore until he spied the cloak and the ugly legs and feet.

"What have we here?" wondered Trinculo, peering at the strange object and poking at it with his toe. "A man, or a fish? Dead or alive? A fish; he smells like a fish; a very ancient and fish-like smell . . ." Thunder growled and threatened again. Trinculo stared about him. There was no shelter anywhere. "Misery acquaints a man with strange bedfellows," he said, and, shutting his eyes and holding his nose, crept under the creature's cloak. Caliban, in mortal terror of the strange spirit, neither spoke nor moved.

Came sounds of a song: not magical in the island's sense, but weavy and peppered with hiccups. A portly fellow in important breeches, waving a bottle like a weapon against flies, came tottering and staggering along the shore. It was Stephano, the King's butler, who had floated to land on a barrel of wine. He kicked against the cloak, not in anger, but because he was too drunk to see it.

"Do not torment me: – O!" came a voice that was thick and harsh. Cautiously Stephano examined the speaking bundle; found it had four legs and no head. Was not surprised. Prodded it.

"Do not torment me, prithee," moaned Caliban, putting out his head. "I'll bring my wood home faster."

Stephano pondered. "He shall taste of my bottle," he said, and thrust it, vaguely, into the hazy, bristly monster's mouth.

"Stephano!" came another voice from the cloak. This was truly uncanny. Stephano flew into a panic. Then Trinculo came out, and the two friends embraced and danced about in their joy at finding each other alive.

Caliban looked on, awed beyond measure by the splendour of the new spirits, and in particular by the one who had given him wine. It seemed to hold a greater enchantment than even Prospero's. "I will kneel to him," whispered Caliban, and crawled humbly towards the ponderous, swaying drunkard. "Hast thou not dropped from heaven?" he asked, staring up at the bottle.

"Out o' the moon," said Stephano; and Caliban believed him.

The drunkard was charmed by his worshipper, and gave him more to drink; but the jester was not pleased. "A most ridiculous monster," he sneered enviously, "to make a wonder of a poor drunkard!"

Nonetheless, off they went together in a staggering bundle, to find where Stephano had hidden his barrel of wine: the butler hiccuping, the jester jeering, and the monster singing and promising his new master all the wonders of the isle. "'Ban, 'Ban, Ca-Caliban," he roared, "has a new master – get a new man!"

A little way from Prospero's dwelling – a rough house of wood, sufficient to keep out the weather and keep in comfort and warmth – the King of Naples' son was carrying logs. Back and forth he toiled, pausing only to wipe the sweat from his brow. He had sworn that he would gladly endure enslavement if only he could see Miranda once a day; and Prospero had put him to the test. Suddenly the house door opened and Miranda, with a quick, backward glance, came running out. "Alas!" she cried, seeing Ferdinand bent, like a beckoning finger, under his heavy burden, "pray you, work not so hard!" She begged him to rest. "My father is hard at study," she promised, with another backward glance. "He's safe for these three hours."

A shadow stirred in the doorway. Prospero was indeed at study, but it was hearts, not books. He smiled at the innocence of his daughter's conspiracy.

"If you'll sit down," urged Miranda, "I'll bear your logs the while."

Ferdinand shook his head. Though the work was heavy, there was pleasure in it: it was not for a harsh master that he laboured, but for a mistress, fair as the sun.

Again Prospero smiled. He had given the young man Caliban's task so that he might seem a Caliban in Miranda's eyes; but Ferdinand laboured willingly and the harsh toil, far from debasing him, had made him seem more noble than before.

"The very instant that I saw you," panted Ferdinand, between logs, "did my heart fly to your service . . ."

"Do you love me?" asked Miranda, more used to plainer speech and hoping she had understood. He did indeed, and told her so again and again; and she, weeping with happiness, confessed the same. Then she left him, for the endless space of half an hour; and he went on heaving logs that seemed as light and airy as dandelion clocks. And Prospero, the hidden observer, shook his head, and sighed, and smiled.

Stephano's wine barrel had been found. He had hidden it beside a stream, under trees. Now he sat astride it, like the king of grapes, while his two subjects squabbled among themselves. Caliban hated Trinculo, who was too familiar with the god of the bottle; and Trinculo despised Caliban because he did not think Stephano worth worshipping.

"Why thou deboshed fish!" jeered Trinculo, as Caliban kissed Stephano's foot.

"Bite him to death, I prithee!" implored Caliban, longing for his new master to dispose of the jester. But Stephano, like a wise ruler, kept the peace; and bent an ear to Caliban who told him of the sorcerer who had stolen the isle.

"Thou liest!" said a voice like Trinculo's. Savagely Caliban turned upon him. Trinculo denied all knowledge of having opened his mouth. Caliban grunted and went on to propose how the isle might be captured by murdering Prospero as he slept.

"Thou liest: thou canst not," said Trinculo's voice again; and again Trinculo denied having spoken. Caliban raged at him, and Stephano warned Trinculo to hold his tongue; and for good measure, and to Caliban's delight, he punched his head.

Even though they were all drunk enough for marvels, it was a strange confusion that had fallen on them, hearing voices when no one spoke; and matters grew stranger still when Stephano began to sing, and was accompanied by mysterious music in the air. The butler and the jester stared at one another aghast. This was more uncanny than anything out of a bottle!

"Be not afeard," urged Caliban, anxious to calm them; "the isle is full of noises, sounds, and sweet airs, that give delight and hurt not . . ."

They took his word for it, and, indeed, as they listened, found a strange pleasure in the music. So much so that, when it began to move away, they rose and, floating on clouds of wine, followed after. This way and that, they went, clinging one to another, as Ariel, the invisible imitator of Trinculo, and the invisible musician to Stephano, led them on. Their conspiracy was as open to Prospero as was the conspiring of Sebastian and Antonio. Plots and murders, greed and cunning were but as waking dreams.

"I can go no further, sir," groaned Gonzalo as the King's party came into a glade that seemed the very image of a glade they had not long left. "I must needs rest me."

The King sighed and took pity on the weary old man, and consented to rest awhile.

"The next advantage will we take thoroughly," breathed Sebastian to Antonio, as their companions sank down exhausted on the grass. His resolve was as firm as ever Antonio could have wished; both men were now eye-deep in thoughts of blood. "I say tonight – "

He fell silent and clutched Antonio by the sleeve; and amazement seized the glade. A rich music had invaded the air. The trees wavered, like trees painted on a veil, became unreal, then seemed to be drawn aside, as if to reveal, briefly, the true face of the haunted isle. Filmy shapes appeared in the air, as if they had always been present, and wanted only clearer sight to be seen. Some had heads like birds, others like wolves, or bears or stags. They were grim in aspect, but gentle in movement. They carried a great table, laden with fruits and meat and tall flagons of wine, which they placed upon the ground; and, with courteous bows and gestures, invited those present to partake of the feast. Then they dissolved, leaving the table behind.

"What were these?" marvelled the King; and he spoke in admiring tones of the gentleness of the spirits.

"Praise in departing," murmured Prospero, the invisible watcher of the scene. For as the hungry lords approached the feast, there was a roar of thunder and a glare of lightning! The glade darkened, there was a thudding of huge wings, and down flew a hideous bird, with the head of a hag and with talons like grappling irons! It perched on the table, clapped its wings, and the feast vanished! Then it turned its red-pouched eyes accusingly on Alonzo, the King of Naples, Sebastian, his brother, and Antonio, Duke of Milan, and shrieked: "You are three men of sin!"

In terror, they drew their swords. Prospero raised his staff. They cried out, staggered, their arms nearly breaking, for their swords were suddenly as heavy as churches! A wild wind began to blow; the trees bent, and the glade seemed enclosed in a dark bubble of tempest. Then the Harpy on the table, in tones that rode the uproar, damned the three men of sin for their old crime against Prospero. It was for this that they were now being punished.

Then lightning blazed again, thunder bellowed, and the Harpy spread its wings and flew away. At once the tempest faded, and the filmy shapes, with the same gentle courtesy as before, returned and bore the table away. Prospero's enemies stared at one another; their faces were grey with guilt.

Prospero nodded. His enemies were within his power. Ariel, in the shape of the Harpy, had done well. Then he remembered Ferdinand, that patient log-bearer, whose back was likely to break before his spirit, and Miranda, who loved him. Swiftly Prospero departed, leaving the glade distracted as the guilty men fled in desperation, and the frightened lords followed anxiously after.

"If I have too austerely punished you," said Prospero, smiling faintly as Miranda nodded and Ferdinand, bruised and aching, stoutly disclaimed, "Your compensation makes amends . . ." Then he revealed that his harshness had been only to test their love and constancy; upon which they smiled modestly, like children who have done well at school. "Sit then," said Prospero, gesturing towards Ferdinand's last log; and, while they sat, side by side, with no eyes but for each other, he summoned Ariel. The great enchanter was not without vanity. Seeing the enchantment in which the lovers held one another, he was stirred to show them that his own power was still greater. Quietly he instructed his servant, who bowed and bowed and sped away. The lovers murmured on. Suddenly there was music in the air, as soft and sweet as any the isle had known. But the lovers murmured on. A strange golden light began to suffuse the grass before them; but the lovers saw only the light in each other's eyes, and still they murmured on.

"No tongue!" commanded Prospero, not without irritation; "all eyes! be silent!"

Guiltily the lovers obeyed; and their eyes grew round with wonderment. Three strange, unearthly women, had stepped out of the air and on to the green stage. They were tall, shining and gracious and robed, it seemed, in softly-coloured vapours. One was Iris, goddess of the rainbow; one was Ceres, goddess of the harvest; and one was Juno, goddess of them all. Ceremoniously they bowed to the lovers and blessed their coming marriage in stately song.

"This is a most majestic vision!" breathed Ferdinand, amazed; and Prospero, gratified by so respectful a response, raised his staff. At once, it was as if the whole world had been an invisible playhouse that had opened its store and tumbled out its richest treasures! A gorgeous crowd of spirits came swirling, dancing out of nowhere, and filled the green: spirits of stream and woodland, of flocks and pastures, smiling nymphs and weird fantastic reapers . . .

Suddenly Prospero stood up. His face was dark with anger! The music faltered and broke up into harsh noises, and the spirits, with looks of dismay, vanished back into the air.

In the midst of his magic, Prospero had remembered Caliban and his murderous plot. The time for it was almost ripe. Then he saw that his sudden anger and the abrupt departure of the vision had distressed the lovers.

"Be cheerful, sir," he urged, taking pity on the confused Ferdinand. "Our revels now are ended ..." He begged the lovers to leave him for a while. He was disturbed, and wished, as he put it, "to still the beating of my mind."

When they had retired, with many a backward glance, into the house, he called Ariel to his side and bade him lay out on a line certain bright and showy garments that were in his possession. He had enchanted a King with an imaginary feast; lovers with imaginary goddesses; for drunkards there was no more need than to lay out fine clothes.

There was a crashing and a stumbling and a blind blundering among the trees as the butler, the jester and the monster drew near the enchanter's house. They had followed the unseen musician through clinging bush and spiteful briar, through filthy ditch and stinking pool, they had lost their bottles, their tempers and their wits, and were as foul and reeking as their thoughts.

"Prithee, my King, be quiet!" warned Caliban, for they were almost at Prospero's dwelling, where murder was to be done. "Give me thy hand," belched Stephano, swaying horribly. "I do begin to have bloody thoughts!" The conspirators put their fingers to their lips, and tottered on.

Suddenly Trinculo saw finery hanging, like executed courtiers, on a line: saw robes and gowns, hats like velvet puddings and wondrous cloaks fit for a duke or a bishop, and instantly saw, in his muddy mind's eye, a Trinculo new-made and marvellous beyond belief.

"Let it alone, thou fool; it is but trash!" cried Caliban, alarmed; but it was too late. Stephano also had been captivated, and was seeing a new Stephano,

43

a glittering, magnificent and even kingly Stephano . . .

"Put off that gown, Trinculo!" he shouted, for the lowly jester had seized on the best one. "Let it alone!" howled Caliban, as his companions began to squabble over the treasures. "Do the murder first!" But they were too busy fighting and struggling and thrusting heads into armholes and making gaudy ghosts with their waving arms, to heed the monster's warning.

Then came a sudden noise of horns and barking dogs. At once, heads came out of sleeves, like conjuror's eggs, and glared palely. Where was the hunt, and who was the quarry? In a moment they knew. Out of the trees there came bounding, with savage eyes and hungry jaws, a pack of huge phantom hounds! The conspirators howled with terror and fled!

Contemptuously, the huntsmen, Prospero and Ariel, urged on the dogs and watched the quarry run.

His enemies were at his mercy, and the time for vengeance was at hand. Soon all would be over, and Ariel would have to be set free. "How fares the King and 's followers?" he asked his impatient, yet everobedient servant. Ariel told him that they had been divided and held in separate enchantments: the King, his brother and Antonio in one place, and the other lords elsewhere. "Him you termed, sir, 'the good old lord Gonzalo'; his tears run down his beard like winter's drops," said the spirit gently. "If you now beheld them, your affections would become tender."

"Dost thou think so, spirit?" asked Prospero, looking strangely at the quick, unearthly creature at his side.

"Mine would, sir, were I human," answered Ariel.

The enchanter bowed his head. The spirit had taught him. Though he had acted like a god, had raised a tempest and brought men to darkest despair, he himself was still human; and vengeance was for

44

the worst, not the best of his kind. "Go release them, Ariel," he commanded. "My charms I'll break, their senses I'll restore."

When his servant had gone, Prospero drew a circle on the ground with his staff. This was to be the last of his magic, his last enchantment. Though he had, in the past, performed huge wonders, had commanded the sun, the sea, and even the dead to obey him, though he had made kings of spirits and ghosts of kings, he had now reached the furthest limits of his power.

He stood aside and concealed himself as Ariel returned, leading the King and all his lords. To the accompaniment of solemn music, the spirit led them into the circle, where at once they were held, like a wooden King and wooden lords, unable to move or to speak. One by one Prospero contemplated them and, as the calming music played, his enemies, fixed in look and attitude, some with arms raised, some with mouths open as if about to speak, seemed less real than dreams.

He sighed and shook his head, and sent Ariel to fetch the sword and hat and robes that he had worn when he was Duke of Milan. Swiftly Ariel returned, and, singing merrily, helped to attire the enchanter until he was exactly that Prospero, Duke of Milan, whom Alonzo, Sebastian and Antonio had treacherously overthrown and believed long dead.

"Why, that's my dainty Ariel!" murmured Prospero, when the task was done. "I shall miss thee!" Then he despatched the spirit to the King's ship, to awaken the sailors from their charmed sleep. As Ariel departed, the solemn music ceased, and the still figures in the circle began to move. They looked about them, rubbed their eyes; then amazement fixed them again. The dead had risen! Before them, in all his

45

familiar dignity, stood Prospero, the rightful Duke of Milan!

Most amiably, even affectionately, the betrayed Duke bade them all welcome. But this was too much for the King, who had long suffered inwardly from the wickedness towards Prospero that he himself had helped to bring about. "Pardon me my wrongs!" he begged, and with all the anguish of true repentance.

But to Prospero, love and gratitude came before forgiveness, and he warmly embraced old Gonzalo, whose kindness towards himself and his helpless child he had never forgotten. The old man stammered out his astonishment and joy; but before he could continue, doubtless into lengthy philosophy, Prospero turned to Sebastian and Antonio. "That brace of lords", as he called them, stood with dread in their eyes. They knew full well that Prospero had seen them through and through, that he had seen not only their villainy towards himself, but also their plot to kill the King. Then Prospero said quietly: "At this time I will tell no tales," and they breathed again. They had been forgiven by silence, which made light of themselves, and left their crimes to weigh upon their hearts.

Last of all, Prospero turned to the King, who still wept for his lost son. Prospero nodded, and confided that he himself had lost a daughter. "O heavens!" cried the King, and wished that he could have died instead, and that his son and Prospero's daughter were alive and King and Queen of Naples. "When did you lose your daughter?"

"In this last tempest," answered Prospero, turning aside to hide his smile. Then he begged the King to enter his house, which, though humble, held a wonder that might well please the King as much as the return of his dukedom pleased Prospero. Doubtfully the King approached. Prospero opened wide the door; and the King cried out! There within sat Ferdinand and Miranda, at play for kingdoms over a game of chess!

"O wonder!" cried Miranda, seeing so many lords and all at once, and each far fairer than Caliban. "How beauteous mankind is! O brave new world, that has such people in it!"

"'Tis new to thee," murmured Prospero, with a suddenly sad smile.

Then the lost son embraced the lost father, and the King discovered that his son and Prospero's daughter were indeed to be married, and his own hopeless hope had been fulfilled, without his having to die for it! Then Ariel brought the sleepy sailors, and there was more amazement, as all had believed each other drowned. "This is as strange a maze as e'er men trod," wondered the King. Prospero begged the King not to trouble his thoughts with the mysteries of the day. Presently he would tell all. He looked about him, as if counting up the number present. He frowned. "There are yet missing of your company," he said, "some few odd lads that you remember not."

The few odd lads, in number, two, and in person, one Stephano, a butler, and one Trinculo, a jester, together with a lumbering, brutish creature that seemed neither fish nor flesh, but stank of both, were driven in by Ariel.

They still wore their stolen finery, but such was the scratched, cramped misery it hung upon, that each seemed a mockery of the other. "Two of these fellows you must know and own," said Prospero. Then, pointing to Caliban, confessed: "This thing of darkness I acknowledge mine."

"How fine my master is!" cried Caliban, seeing Prospero in ducal robes; and straightway transferred his allegiance to the better man. "What a thrice-double ass was I, to take this drunkard for a god, and worship this dull fool!" No hint of contradiction came from his companions; they were too sore to do anything but admit the truth.

Prospero dismissed them, and with no worse punishment than to put back what they had stolen. Then Prospero renewed his invitation to the King to enter his house, where he would tell him all, and, in the morning, sail with him to Naples, for the wedding of their children; after which, he himself would retire to his dukedom of Milan.

"I'll deliver all," he assured the King; "and promise you calm seas, auspicious gales ... My Ariel, chick," he murmured to his hovering, beloved servant, "that is thy charge; then to the elements be free, and fare thou well!" Ariel laughed; and then, with a thousand thousand bows that made a shining circle round the enchanter, the spirit fled.

That night, when all had retired to bed, Prospero stood by the sea, a tall and lonely figure, silvered by starlight. First his magic mantle, then his magic book, and last of all his staff, broken in two, he cast into the waves. He had no more need of them, nor of the enchanted isle. By his art he had made men see themselves, and, through make-believe, come to truth. Now he, too, like Ariel and Caliban, longed to be free.

The Merchant of Venice

In the watery city of Venice, where high-necked boats, like children's painted horses, nod and curtsey along the flowing streets, and the bright air is full of the winks and chinks of smiling money, there lived a merchant by the name of Antonio. He was as good and upright a man as ever merchant was, and all his wealth was laid out in tall, billowing vessels that ventured for trade far and wide.

He had everything a merchant might have wished for; but he was melancholy and knew not why. It was as if there was a shadow over the sun, cooling his pleasures and darkening his days. As he strolled along the busy Rialto, where rich men gathered in their velvet caps and brocaded gowns and talked of affairs, two friends tried to discover the cause of his sadness, and so cure it. Was he troubled about the safety of his vessels? Or was he in love, which was a mournful business if ever there was one? He shook his head.

As they walked, they were joined by three young men, dressed in the height of silken fashion. Their names were Bassanio, Lorenzo and Gratiano, and at first sight there seemed little else to choose between them. They were three young men with nothing better to do than to stroll, and talk, and laugh and enjoy being young.

"You look not well, Signior Antonio," observed

49

Gratiano, who was the liveliest of the three, "you have too much respect upon the world . . ."

The merchant disclaimed; and Gratiano rattled on, nineteen to the dozen, if not twenty, until even he became wearied of his own chatter. Linking arms with Lorenzo, he drifted away after the others, who had already gone. The merchant and Bassanio were left alone.

"Gratiano speaks an infinite deal of nothing," said Bassanio, falling into seriousness as if out of respect for his companion's grave looks.

Antonio smiled. He was deeply fond of Bassanio and looked upon him almost as a son. It often happens with older men, whose sober lives are lined and straitened in with affairs of business, that they look fondly on the happy carelessness of youth, as they might take pleasure in the spring time's birds.

There was a lady that Bassanio had talked of, and had promised to speak of again. Antonio inquired about her but Bassanio shook his head. He carried too heavy a cargo of present troubles to spread his sails for love. He had spent all his rich inheritance and was drowning in a sea of debts.

"To you, Antonio," he confessed, "I owe the most in money and in love . . ."

Antonio bade him not think of it. It grieved the good merchant to see the carefree young man grow grey and pinched for the want of so mean a thing as money.

"My purse, my person," he offered impulsively, "my extremest means lie all unlocked to your occasions."

Bassanio needed no more invitation. If but Antonio would lend him what he needed for a certain enterprise, then Bassanio was confident all would be repaid. The merchant smiled at the young man's enthusiasm, and asked what the certain enterprise might be? Bassanio hesitated; and sighed.

"In Belmont," said he, with an ardent look, "is a lady richly left . . ." Not only was this lady as lovely as she was rich, but she was jewelled with every virtue; and suitors came from far and wide to gain her heart and hand. "Her name is Portia," said Bassanio, as if in that name was enshrined all the beauty of the world. He had seen her once and had received such encouragement from her eyes that he was sure he would succeed in winning her. That is, if only he had the money to present himself before her as a suitor of equal worth among his rivals.

Antonio nodded. Maybe it was not an enterprise that a sober merchant would have embarked upon, but it seemed proper for a youth like Bassanio, who was made, not for trade, but for love.

"Thou know'st," he began, "that all my fortunes are at sea; neither have I money nor commodity to raise a present sum." Here, Bassanio began to look dismayed. Antonio continued: "Therefore go forth, try what my credit can in Venice do. Go presently inquire (and so will I) where money is . . ."

Bassanio beamed. His eyes shone with tears of gratitude. Antonio was his good angel. He shook him warmly by the hand and sped away to find some worthy man from whom he might borrow money against Antonio's good name. Antonio gazed affectionately after him as he hastened, like a bright dream, among the sombrely robed men of business who thronged the Rialto. Presently he was gone, and the merchant's strange melancholy returned . . .

Far across the sea in Belmont, the Lady Portia's palace was besieged by sighs. Suitors drooped and languished, sad as urn draperies, in her doorways, in her gardens, in her stables, and in her wine vaults.

"By my troth, Nerissa," she confided to her maid, being weighed down by all this forlorn furniture, and shadowed by a strange condition laid upon her by her dead father that she should never choose a husband but must instead be chosen, "my little body is aweary of this great world."

Portia's hair was fair as sunshine and her countenance was fairer still. In stature she was, perhaps, a finger's breadth below the middle height; but such was the grace of her form that, beside her, those of the middle height seemed too tall. Whoever gained her love would never want for sunny days, nor a dearer summer than hers. Yet this fair lady could only be won by lottery. By her dying father's decree her fate was locked in one of three caskets, of gold, of silver, and of lead. One choice was allowed each suitor. If he chose wrongly, that was the end of his hopes.

"What warmth is there in your affection towards any one of these princely suitors that are already come?" asked Nerissa, curious to learn if her mistress's heart inclined any one way more than another.

"I pray thee over-name them," said Portia with a yawn.

"First there is the Neapolitan prince."

The lady wrinkled her nose.

"He doth nothing but talk of his horse, and he makes it a great appropriation to his own good parts that he can shoe him himself; I am much afeard my lady his mother played false with a smith."

Nerissa laughed.

"Then there is the County Palatine."

"He doth nothing but frown," complained Portia, "he hears merry tales and smiles not. I had rather be married to a death's head with a bone in his mouth."

Nerissa agreed with her young mistress. Belmont was a house of smiles.

"How say you by the French lord, Monsieur Le Bon?"

"God made him," pronounced Portia, "and therefore let him pass for a man." Nothing more, it seemed, could be said in favour of Monsieur Le Bon.

"What say you then to Falconbridge, the young baron of England?"

"You know I say nothing to him, for he understands not me, nor I him . . . alas! who can converse with a dumb-show?"

The other suitors fared no better in Portia's esteem; there was a Scottish lord who did nothing but quarrel and brawl, and a German duke who did nothing but drink. "I will do anything, Nerissa," wailed Portia, quite overcome by the thought of the wine-swilling duke, "ere I will be married to a sponge."

But Portia's fears proved groundless. Her present crop of suitors was departing and there was none who cared to risk his fortune on the lottery of the caskets.

"Do you not remember lady," said Nerissa suddenly, "in your father's time, a Venetian (a scholar and a soldier) that came hither in company of the Marquis of Montferrat?"

Portia frowned; then her eyes gleamed brightly.

"Yes, yes, it was Bassanio, as I think so was he called."

"True madam, he of all the men that ever my foolish eyes looked upon was the best deserving a fair lady."

"I remember him well," murmured Portia, smiling to herself, "and I remember him worthy of thy praise."

In Venice, Bassanio had laid his hands on money. He had found a man who might be willing to lend him money against the word and bond of his friend Antonio. In a narrow street, where the water ran dark and crooked between high weeping walls, and little barred windows, like imprisoned eyes, stared dully down, he had met with a lean, bearded man in black, who smiled and frowned and smiled and frowned, and rubbed his hands together as if he would get to the bone of them. Shylock was his name, and he was a Jew.

He was not a man to Bassanio's liking, nor to the liking of any Venetian, for he seemed to crawl across the fair fabric of the city like a spider, spoiling it. But he lent money.

"Three thousand ducats, well," mused the Jew, rubbing his hands and frowning in his beard.

"Aye, sir, for three months," urged Bassanio, hovering brightly in attendance on the dark, ugly Jew.

"Three thousand ducats for three months, and Antonio bound," brooded the Jew, beginning to pace back and forth with such nervous rapidity that Bassanio was hard put to keep up with him.

Shylock was doubtful. He allowed that Antonio was a good man, meaning that the merchant's credit was good – that being the only way by which a merchant's goodness was to be measured – but all his wealth was laid out in ships at sea, and, as the Jew put it, "ships are but boards, sailors but men . . . there is the peril of waters, winds and rocks."

He shook his head; and poor Bassanio looked dismayed. He sighed; and Bassanio's heart dropped fathoms deep. Then he chuckled; and Bassanio walked on air!

"Three thousand ducats," said the Jew, most cheerfully. "I think I may take his bond . . . May I speak with Antonio?"

"If it please you to dine with us," offered Bassanio eagerly.

The Jew took a pace back. He stared at Bassanio as if he was mad.

"Yes, to smell pork," he answered savagely. "I will buy with you, sell with you, talk with you, walk with you, and so following; but I will not eat with you, drink with you, nor pray with you . . ."

A figure approached.

"This is Signior Antonio," said Bassanio quickly. He was fearful that he might have, unwittingly, offended the lender of money. With an anxious watch upon the Jew (lest he lose him), the young man went a few paces to meet the merchant, who was plainly pleased to have found his friend. Shylock, shrinking back against the wall till he seemed no more than an ugly stain upon it, stared at the merchant.

"How like a fawning publican he looks!" he snarled into his beard. "I hate him for he is a Christian." Nor was this the only reason for the Jew's hate. The merchant lent money without interest, and so brought down the cost of borrowing in Venice. Money was the Jew's only commodity, and the Christian undermined him. The Christian could make money out of trade; the Jew, by Venetian law, could only make money out of money. Take away his money and you take away his life. For these reasons the dark Jew hated the bright Christians of Venice; and strongest of all, he hated them because they hated him. Hate breeds hate as fast as summer flies.

But nothing of this hatred showed as he greeted the merchant with smiles and bows and outstretched palms. All was satin courtesy. Antonio, on the other hand, regarded the cringing Jew with unconcealed contempt. He loathed and despised the Jew and, had it not been for the purpose of supplying the need of his young friend, who looked anxiously from one to the other, he would have scorned to walk upon the same side of the street as Shylock.

"Three thousand ducats," said Shylock, "'tis a good round sum. Three months from twelve, then let me see the rate."

"Well, Shylock," demanded the merchant coldly, "shall we be beholding to you?"

The Jew smiled humbly; and sighed.

"Signior Antonio, many a time and oft in the Rialto you have rated me about my moneys and my usances; still have I borne it with a patient shrug, for suff'r-ance is the badge of all our tribe. You call me misbeliever, cut-throat dog, and spat upon my Jewish gaberdine . . . Well then, it now appears you need my help . . . 'Shylock, we would have moneys,' you say so . . . What should I say to you? Should I not say 'Hath a dog money? Is it possible a cur can lend three thousand ducats?' or shall I bend low, and in a bondman's key . . . say this: 'Fair sir, you spat on me on Wednesday last . . . another time you called me dog: and for these courtesies I'll lend you thus much moneys'?"

"I am as like to call thee so again," said Antonio contemptuously; for the Jew's long drawn out com-plainings had seemed to the upright merchant – whose affairs were open to the world – no better than the needless whining of a cur. Angrily, for he could see that his young friend was worried, he went on to demand a plain answer. Would the Jew, or would he not, lend the money? If the money was to be lent, then let it be done according to a bond. If the bond was broken, then the penalty must be exacted. Anto-nio desired no favours from the Jew.

"Why look how you storm!" cried Shylock, shrink-ing before the merchant's anger as before a task-master's whip. "I would be friends with you," he pleaded; and then, to prove his good faith, offered to lend the money and demand not a jot of interest.

"This were kindness!" cried Bassanio, as the pros-pect of going to Belmont with servants in attendance and fine clothes on his back seemed within his grasp.

Shylock, now friends with everybody (though none

was friends with him), nodded and nodded and rubbed his skinny hands. They must go at once to a notary and draw up the bond. Though there was to be no interest, it was proper that there should be a bond, to be exacted only if the money lent was not repaid. And what should that bond be? Not property, not furnishings, not jewels, but — here the Jew laughed merrily, and the high-pitched sound made the barred windows seem to look sharply down – but a pound of the merchant's living flesh! And why not? Was not money flesh and life to the Jew? Why not then to the merchant? Shylock smiled at the humour of it with all the openness at his command. But smiles and snarls were kissing cousins to his lips. Antonio stared. Then he shrugged his shoulders and smiled. The Jew's humour was as strange as the Jew. He was content to seal the bargain which seemed, to him, far-fetched in the extreme.

"You shall not seal to such a bond for me," muttered Bassanio, suddenly uneasy for his friend.

But Antonio brushed aside his friend's concern: his ships and his money would all be home again a month before the bond was due. Shylock also was eager to quiet Bassanio's fears.

"If he should break his day what should I gain by exaction of the forfeiture?" he demanded. "A pound of man's flesh taken from a man, is not so estimable, profitable neither as flesh of muttons, beefs or goats." No, no, it was only to oblige Antonio and be his friend that he had proposed so unthrifty a bond.

The merchant believed him – and why not? What manner of man could really desire flesh instead of ducats?

"Hie thee gentle Jew," he laughed, as Shylock scuttled away to gather in the ducats, "the Hebrew will turn Christian, he grows kind."

But Bassanio shook his head. "I like not fair terms and a villain's mind."

Antonio smiled, and once more brushed aside his young friend's fears and forebodings.

Now Shylock had a daughter called Jessica, and she was as lovely as the night in Spring. Her mother must have been most wondrous for the daughter to have come by so much beauty, though mixed with Shylock's blood. She longed with all her heart to fly from the Jew's dark house, not to freedom, but to the prettier prison of love. She loved Lorenzo, Bassanio's friend, and he loved her, though all that had passed between them had been sighs from a window and sighs from the street. Nor was she alone in longing to escape from Shylock. The Jew had a servant by name of Launcelot Gobbo who likewise pined. He was a lively youth, and could no longer endure the miserly life of locks and bolts, and keys and strongboxes, and rooms that never saw the light of day.

He was the first to fly away. He took his chance when it came, which was when Bassanio called to leave a letter, bidding the Jew come to supper with Antonio. Launcelot begged to be taken into Bassanio's service, which Bassanio gladly did, for he had need of a servant now that he was to go to Belmont and try his fortune with the lady there. Gratiano, that idle talker, strolling by took it into his head (where there was room enough and to spare), to ask if he, too, might go to Belmont with Bassanio. Bassanio sighed. It was hard to refuse a friend, but harder still to oblige such a one. He pleaded that, if Gratiano came, he would behave with proper modesty, for the fair lady of Belmont would surely not look kindly on a suitor who came with a chattering idiot in his train.

Sweet Jessica was as miserable as a widowed jackdaw when Launcelot told her of his good luck.

She grieved that her father's hated house would now be robbed of its only cheerfulness.

"But fare thee well," she wished him, "there is a ducat for thee . . ."

She gave him the gold and, in addition, with much secrecy gave him a letter for his new master's friend, the handsome Lorenzo. When Launcelot had gone she sighed most bitterly, for she was ashamed that she was her father's child. "O Lorenzo," she whispered, "if thou keep promise I shall end this strife, become a Christian and thy loving wife!"

Young Launcelot, who loved and pitied his old master's daughter with all his heart, delivered the letter as swiftly as he could. Eagerly Lorenzo read it. His eyes shone, his heart soared. The letter was such a letter as lovers dream of. His Jessica was waiting for him. She had gathered together a dowry of gold and jewels, and was waiting for him to come and take her from her father's house.

It was a night of carnival. Flutes and songs and drums enriched the warm air. Slow gondolas, heavy with lovers, like baskets crammed with grapes, drifted between the mansions, looped and necklaced with little lights. Strange, fantastic figures, led by torch bearers, danced and capered along the water-streets, and mocked at their mirror images as they kept rippled pace. Masks and laughter were the order of the night, save in one dark street and in one dark house where the Jew, Shylock, lived.

The door opened, and Shylock came out. His eyes glittered angrily as he heard the sounds of distant music and light laughter. He called for his daughter and she came, gleaming softly, like a candle.

"I am bid forth to supper Jessica," he said. "There are my keys . . ." She took the heavy ring, which, with its dull iron garnishings, hung on her white arm like a manacle on a moonbeam. "Jessica my girl," said the father, caught by a sudden dread, "look to my house. I am right loath to go, there is some ill a-brewing towards my rest, for I did dream of money-bags tonight."

He shivered in his long black gown; then a louder burst of music made him angry again. "Lock up my doors," he commanded, as sounds of singing and dancing feet drew near. "Clamber not you up to the casements then nor thrust your head into the public street to gaze on Christian fools with varnished faces." He shook his head. "I have no mind of feasting forth tonight: but I will go . . ."

Breathing deeply with relief, Jessica watched her father go, his dark shape putting out the distant lights, like a cloud among stars. Then she went back within doors.

Presently two friends of Lorenzo came by. They paused, looked up at the house, and nodded. This was the place where they were to meet. They waited, murmuring mockingly of lovers being late. Then Lorenzo came. All three wore painted masks with painted smiles that hid . . . more smiles. So that one might have wondered which were faces, which were masks. Lorenzo gazed up towards a casement that was stoutly shuttered. He called softly:

"Ho! Who's within?"

The shutters opened and a light shone out, and in that light was Jessica. Pretty Jessica, anxiously disguised in costume of a boy. She looked down, saw the painted smiler looking up.

"Who are you?"

"Lorenzo and thy love!"

She laughed for joy and then, bidding him catch, cast down, like a bright tear from her father's house, a casket of jewels and gold. Then she vanished from the window to lock the doors and fill her purse and boy's pockets with all the ducats she could carry away. So she left her father's scowls for love's smiles, and her father's darkness for love's light, taking with her his treasure and herself, who was the dearest treasure of all.

That very night, in a close and secret gondola, Lorenzo and Jessica fled from the city and Shylock's wrath. At the same time, or very near it, Bassanio with his friend Gratiano, and attended by Launcelot Gobbo his new servant, embarked for Belmont and its lady. He carried with him the love and fond hopes of Antonio the merchant who, for Bassanio's sake, had pledged his very life to the Jew.

Even as the casket that Jessica had thrown down from Shylock's window had contained her father's treasure, so one of the three closed caskets in Belmont contained another father's treasure: not gold, not jewels, but his daughter herself. In one of them was locked fair Portia's likeness, and he who chose it would gain her hand and heart. But in which casket? The gold, the silver, or the lead? That was the question. To choose right meant happiness beyond measure; to choose wrong meant, by the harsh condition imposed on the chooser, to go forever without a wife.

Soft lutes played delicate airs in the silken chamber where the caskets were, for a new suitor had come to Belmont to try for the lady. The Prince of Morocco, a turbaned Moor whose dark face sprang from his rich attire like ebony from snow. That he loved fair Portia was not to be doubted, for he was willing to risk all on the chance of winning her. While Portia and her maids looked uncertainly on, wondering where he would choose, he studied the three caskets, each in turn, as if his fierce eyes would probe the metal and spy the treasure within.

"This first of gold," murmured the dark Prince, "who this inscription bears, 'Who chooseth me shall gain what many men desire.' The second silver, which this promise carries, 'Who chooseth me shall get as much as he deserves.' This third, dull lead, with warning all as blunt, 'Who chooseth me must give and hazard all he hath.'" He shook his head.

"The one of them contains my picture, Prince," said Portia softly, "if you choose that then I am yours withal."

He flashed upon her a smile like dark fruit sliced; then returned to his contemplation of the caskets. Not lead, never lead. "Is't like that lead contains her?" he wondered. "'Twere damnation to think so base a thought!" But what of silver? "O sinful thought!" he exclaimed, "never so rich a gem was set in worse than gold!" He picked up the golden casket. "Deliver me the key!" he demanded, his deep voice shaking with expectation. "Here do I choose . . ."

"There take it Prince," said Portia quietly, "and if my form lies there then I am yours!"

He took the key and unlocked the casket. He looked within. A grey pallor over-washed his dark complexion. Not fair Portia but a Death's head glared up at him. He had lost all. He took his sad departure with dignity and some nobility.

"A gentle riddance," breathed Portia, much relieved, for, though she had admired the Prince, she had not loved him. "Draw the curtains, go."

In Venice, in busy, monied Venice, all was confusion. The Jew had discovered the loss of his daughter and the loss of his gold. He was mad with dismay, not knowing which loss had plunged the sharper dagger in his heart.

"I never heard a passion so confused," marvelled a friend of Antonio's to another, "as the dog Jew did utter in the streets – 'My daughter! O my ducats! O my daughter! Fled with a Christian! O my Christian ducats! Justice, the law . . .'"

As the other listened to the tale of the Jew's wild destruction, he stook his head gravely. "Let good Antonio look he keep his day," he murmured, "or he shall pay for this."

Upon which his companion remembered, as people often do when there's a chance of disaster for others, that he'd heard a rumour that one of Antonio's ships had been wrecked. The two gentlemen stared at one another, and then with words, if not with hearts, expressed their deep concern for what might befall their friend Antonio if he failed to keep his bond.

In Belmont, where the concerns of Venice were as distant as the moon, another suitor had come to try for Portia's hand. A Spanish gentleman, gorgeous in velvet and with a hand and wrist as proud as a swan's neck. The Prince of Arragon, no less. While Portia and Nerissa and the bowing servants of the Prince looked on, the nobleman himself surveyed the caskets and the prize. Modestly Portia lowered her eyes, and hid a smile.

The leaden basket detained him not an instant: so princely a hand was never formed to touch so base a metal. Gold he toyed with, then put it by, for the good reason that it promised "what many men desire". "I will not choose what many men desire," he said, with a curl of his lip and a wave of his hand, "because I will not jump with common spirits, and rank me with the barbarous multitudes." The servants bowed and murmured admiringly, while Portia and Nerissa cast their eyes to heaven. So to the silver casket he turned. "'Who chooseth me shall get as much as he deserves'." He smiled knowingly and his servants nodded at their master's sagacity. What could such a prince as he deserve, but the very best? "Give me a key for this," he commanded, with a snap of his fingers and a waiting hand, "and instantly unlock my fortunes here."

The casket was opened, and the Prince looked within. He was silent. At such a moment the Moor's complexion had turned to grey; this Prince's colour darkened to red, and all his servants trembled.

"What's here?" he demanded at length, "the portrait of a blinking idiot." Anger gave way to grief. "Did I deserve no more than a fool's head?" he asked of the lady who most unkindly smiled. "Is that my prize?"

"To offend and judge are distinct offices," said Portia, a little sorry for the downcast Prince, "and of opposed natures."

He sighed heavily; but before he took his departure, he mustered up his spirits sufficiently to admit, "With one fool's head I came to woo, but I go away with two."

When the Prince and all his servants had departed, there came news that yet another suitor was approaching. His messenger, a young Venetian was already at the gate. Portia and Nerissa looked at one another. Who could this messenger's master be?

"Bassanio," prayed Nerissa, "Lord Love, if thy will it be!"

The water ran choppily by the Rialto, as an invisible wind, like strong rumour, sent it scurrying. Two good friends of Antonio talked solemnly, amid the bustle and business of brokers and merchants. Again they'd heard tales that one of Antonio's ships had been wrecked and all its cargo lost. They shook their heads sadly over their friend's ill-luck, and prayed there would be no more of it.

"How now Shylock!" exclaimed one, as the Jew drew near, "what news among the merchants?"

The Jew, his eyes all red from weeping, glared at the Christian gentlemen, in whose contemptuous smiles he read, all too easily, mockery for his loss. His daughter was gone, and they laughed at him. Such a daughter, they jeered, was too good for such a father to keep. "But tell us," they asked, brushing aside the Jew's misfortunes, "do you hear whether Antonio have had any loss at sea or no?"

Another knife in his heart, for Antonio was in distress and near to being bankrupt. More ducats thrown to the dogs! "Let him look to his bond," snarled Shylock, "let him look to his bond!"

"Why," cried one of the gentlemen, in some surprise, "I am sure if he forfeit thou wilt not take his flesh – what's that good for?"

"To bait fish withal," screamed the Jew, beside himself with grief and rage, "if it will feed nothing else, it will feed my revenge."

The two gentlemen stepped back; passers-by paused; velvet lords and ladies turned, stared, exchanged glances of scorn (but discreetly for none wanted to be noticed and publicly pounced upon by the inflamed Jew), as the black-gowned Shylock raved on: "He hath disgraced me and hindered me half a million, laughed at my losses, mocked at my gains, scorned my nation, thwarted my bargains, cooled my friends, heated mine enemies. And what's his reason? I am a Jew." Here, the money-lender glared about him with such ferocious distress and such ancient anguish, that the brightly hovering world of Venice seemed to shrink and tremble, like butterflies' wings at the cooling of summer. Shylock went on, his voice as raw as the shrieking of sea birds: "Hath not a Jew eyes? Hath not a Jew hands, organs, dimensions, senses, affections, passions? fed with the same food, hurt by the same weapons, subject to the same diseases, healed by the same means, warmed and cooled by the same winter and summer as a Christian is? If you prick us do we not bleed? If you tickle us do we not laugh? If you poison us do we not die? And if you wrong us shall we not revenge? If a Jew wrong a Christian, what is his humility? revenge! If a Christian wrong a Jew, what should his sufferance be by Christian example? Why revenge! The villainy you teach me I will execute, and it shall go hard but I will better the instruction."

Shylock stopped, panting from his exertions. To the relief of Antonio's friends, a messenger came, bidding them come to the merchant's house. The lookers-on shrugged their shoulders and strolled away. Shylock stood alone, until another of his tribe, one Tubal, joined him.

"What news from Genoa?" demanded Shylock. "Hast thou found my daughter?"

The news was bad. Tubal had heard of her but not seen her. Shylock was plunged into the blackest misery. All his riches gone. Would that his daughter was dead! "The curse never fell upon our nation till now," he groaned, "I never felt it till now . . ."

But, on the other hand, there was news in Genoa that one of Antonio's ships had been cast away. Ah! That was better! Yet then again, Tubal had heard, in talkative Genoa, that Shylock's daughter had spent, at one sitting, four score ducats.

"Thou stick'st a dagger in me," moaned Shylock.

But, said Tubal, Antonio's creditors were gathering, and the Jew was pacified – until he heard that one of them had had a ring off Jessica for a monkey.

"Out upon her!" wept Shylock, wringing his hands and tearing at the shiny ringlets of his hair, "it was my turquoise, I had it of Leah when I was a bachelor;

I would not have given it for a wilderness of monkeys!"

But, thank God, Antonio was ruined, and Shylock sent Tubal for an officer to enforce his terrible claim upon the proud merchant who had spurned him.

In Belmont, in smiling Belmont, the new suitor had appeared; and to Portia's joy and fear he was that very Bassanio she remembered from long ago: to her joy because her heart danced to see him, and to her fear because, if he failed in his choice of casket, she would never see him more. In vain she begged him put off the fateful choice, and take pleasure in her house and gardens, and the soft air of Belmont, which was always filled with music; but Bassanio, having come thus far, and at such a cost, could not endure to delay. So now he stood before the caskets, with Gratiano (strangely quiet Gratiano), by his side; and the fair lady of Belmont, with all her maids like pale daisies bending towards her warmth and light, watched him intently. Softly, though in a voice that trembled, Portia bade a page boy, who sat cross-legged and fondled a lute almost as large as himself, to sing. The child frowned down at his instrument, and gravely began: "Tell me where is Fancy bred, or in the heart or in the head?"

Some say it was the song that guided Bassanio in his choice, for Portia already loved him well enough to give his fortune a proper turn; but she was ever honourable in her dealings, and well Bassanio knew it. No! If he was guided at all, it was not by rhyme, but by the bright sudden looks of Portia's sea-blue eyes, which warned him that true beauty dwells within. It was his own love and hers that taught him the wisdom to know where his best hope lay: not in gold, not in silver, but in quiet, unassuming lead.

"And here choose I," he breathed. "Joy be the consequence!"

And so it was. Within the leaden casket was fair Portia's portrait. Bassanio had won the lady of his heart. The joy of the chosen was no less than the joy of the chooser; they were a pair fairly matched. To solemnize their promised marriage, Portia gave Bassanio a ring, and made him swear that he would never, so long as he loved her, part with it. (Such a ring Leah had given to Shylock, and Jessica had stolen it away.) Willingly Bassanio promised. And then Gratiano spoke up: he too had found a bride, whose promise had depended on the choice of casket. She was Portia's maid, Nerissa, whose loveliness was only exceeded by her mistress's as the lily by the rose. It would seem that, by holding his tongue in accordance with his promise, Gratiano had made a better conquest by silence than by talk.

Then, in the midst of this high summer of happiness, a cloud came over the sun. There arrived from Venice Lorenzo and Jessica, and a friend of Antonio's. They brought a letter from the merchant to his young friend.

"Sweet Bassanio," wrote the merchant, in the extremity of his distress, "my ships have all miscarried, my creditors grow cruel, my estate is very low, my bond to the Jew is forfeit, and, since in paying it, it is impossible I should all live, debts are cleared between you and I, if I might but see you at my death; notwithstanding, use your pleasure; if your love do not persuade you to come, let not my letter."

Belmont was fallen into dullness. The house was quiet and the gardens emptied. Lutes and guitars were coffined in their cases, for the two new brides had been widowed by the need of a friend. Their husbands, Bassanio and Gratiano, had hastened to

Venice to try to save the good Antonio. But there was little hope. Even though Portia had urged Bassanio to offer the Jew many times the value of the bond, it was feared he would not take it. His daughter Jessica declared that she had heard her father swear that there was no money that could buy back the bond. His love of ducats had been quite swallowed up in his desire for revenge. He would have his pound of flesh. He knew full well that not even the Duke could deny him this; for the bond had been drawn up in accordance with the law of Venice, and to skirt that law would be to undermine it, and so undermine the chief strength of the state.

Portia thought deeply about these matters, and wondered how she might help her husband's friend with her wit if her wealth proved to be of no avail. It was a matter of law, and, though no lawyer herself, she had a cousin in Padua, by name of Doctor Bellario, who was most learned in the science. To Bellario, then, she sent her servant with a letter requiring certain notes and articles of clothing to be dispatched to the Venice ferry, where she and her maid would receive them. Then, confiding to Lorenzo and Jessica the charge of her house, she gave out that she and Nerissa were retiring to a monastery while their husbands were away. This done, she and Nerissa left Belmont on their strange adventure.

"Come on, Nerissa," she murmured, with brightly gleaming eyes, "I have work in hand that you yet know not of; we'll see our husbands before they think of us!"

The waters of Venice ran dark and deep beside the Hall of Justice, reflecting stone walls and no more than a knife of the sky. Within, among gilded pillars and richly tapestried walls, from which long-dead law-givers gazed faintly down, there was much murmuring as the Duke and all the dignitaries of the State entered to hear the cause and give judgement. They sat, with a sigh of crimson velvets and a quiet chiming of their chains of gold. Antonio was summoned and duly fetched. Poor man! his face was already as pale as death. He saw Bassanio among the onlookers, and seemed to gain a little courage from the presence of his young friend.

"Go one and call the Jew into the court," commanded the Duke, Shylock was called; and Shylock came. In Sabbath gown, as black as night, he stood before the court, rubbing and rubbing his thin white hands, as the Duke urged him to be merciful and not demand the terrible payment of the bond. Shylock shook his head, and his oiled locks gleamed redly in the crowding candlelight, as if his bloody thoughts had stained them. He would have his bond. He stared defiantly at the assembled lords in all their pride. "If you deny it," he warned, "let the danger light upon your charter and your city's freedom!"

Impulsively Bassanio stepped forward and pleaded with the Jew. Shylock answered him coldly, curtly, and scarce deigning to look at him. Antonio interposed and begged Bassanio not waste his breath. "Make no more offers," he pleaded, weary with distress, "let me have judgement and the Jew his will."

"For thy three thousand ducats here is six!" cried Bassanio, throwing down a heavy purse on to the table of judgement. Again Shylock shook his head. He would have nothing but his bond.

"How shalt thou hope for mercy rend'ring none?" wondered the Duke, shocked beyond measure by the force of the Jew's hatred.

"What judgement shall I dread doing no wrong?" demanded Shylock, angry with this Christian court that sought to escape its own laws. "If you deny me," he cried, "fie upon your law! There is no force in the decrees of Venice: I stand for judgement; answer, shall I have it?"

The Duke and his lords gravely conferred. There was no doubt that the Jew had law upon his side. If only the learned Doctor Bellario, for whom the Duke had sent, would come and unperplex the court! Then, even as that doctor's name was spoken, it was learned that he had sent a messenger with letters . . .

"Bring us the letters!" exclaimed the Duke, "call the messenger!"

The messenger was called, and the messenger came: a most curious small clerk, in clerk's gown, and clerk's hat, with clerk's wig and clerk's spectacles, so that nothing showed but what was proper to a clerk, who did not look like Nerissa at all. In a voice that struggled to keep low, but kept rising, like a swimmer for air, the clerk presented the Duke with Doctor Bellario's greetings, and his letters. As the Duke read the letters, the court buzzed with expectation; then sharply drew in its breath as it was seen that Shylock, merciless Shylock, had taken out his knife and was steadily sharpening it against the sole of his shoe.

Doctor Bellario's letters told that he was sick and unable to attend; but that, in his place, he had sent a young lawyer in whom he had the greatest faith. The Duke looked up, and there before him stood the young lawyer: a most curious small young lawyer, in lawyer's gown and lawyer's hat, with lawyer's wig and lawyer's thick spectacles so that nothing showed but what was proper to a lawyer, who did not look like fair Portia at all. The Duke looked doubtfully at the little advocate, whose chin, nestling in lawyer's bands, was as beardless as silk. Was the young lawyer acquainted with the cause before the court? The young lawyer was; and the young lawyer's voice was not unlike the clerk's, being low in parts. The

Duke shrugged his shoulders and, with a wave of his many-ringed hand, indicated that the trial between the Jew and the merchant of Venice should proceed.

"Of a strange nature is the suit you follow," said the lawyer to the Jew, "yet in such rule that the Venetian law cannot impugn you as you do proceed . . ." The Jew's beard revealed, rather than hid, the grimness of his smile. "Do you confess the bond?" asked the lawyer of the merchant. Helplessly the merchant confessed it. "Then must the Jew be merciful," decided the lawyer.

"On what compulsion must I?" demanded the Jew. "Tell me that!" The court murmured. What compulsion could this small lawyer bring upon the dark, threatening Jew to make him merciful? The lawyer faced the Jew; took a pace towards him; held out hands in a gesture of pleading – hands that were whiter and gentler than lawyer's hands ever were; and spoke to him:

"The quality of mercy is not strained, it droppeth as the gentle rain from heaven upon the place beneath; it is twice blessed, it blesseth him that gives, and him that takes, 'tis mightiest in the mightiest, it becomes the throned monarch better than his crown . . ." Thus the lawyer pleaded with Shylock to temper justice with mercy. But Shylock, savage Shylock, would have nothing of it. He demanded his pound of the merchant's flesh.

"Is he not able to discharge the money?" inquired the lawyer of the court.

"Yes, here I tender it for him in the court!" cried Bassanio, and offered twice the sum, or even ten times (upon which the small lawyer looked sharply at the young man who was so prodigal with ducats), to redeem the bond. "If that will not suffice," went on Bassanio, "it must appear that malice bears down truth. Wrest once the law to your authority; to do a great right, do a little wrong, and curb this cruel devil of his will."

"It must not be," said the lawyer, "there is no power in Venice can alter a decree established: 'twill be recorded for a precedent . . ."

"A Daniel come to judgement: yea, a Daniel!" cried Shylock, capering with delight to find the justice of his cause upheld. "O wise young judge how I do honour thee!"

The small lawyer nodded, and asked to see the bond. It was given and, when read, proved to be as the Jew had said.

"Take thrice thy money, bid me tear the bond," urged the lawyer. But Shylock would not relent. He stood by the law, and the law upheld him. Antonio must pay the forfeit: a pound of his living flesh, to be cut nearest his heart.

"The law allows it, and the court awards it," decreed the lawyer. So Antonio, condemned Antonio, took his last farewell of Bassanio and prepared himself for Shylock's upraised knife. The court leaned forward, pale with dread at what the law could do.

"Tarry a little," said the lawyer suddenly, even as the knife was at Antonio's breast, "there is something else. This bond doth give thee here no jot of blood, the words expressly are 'a pound of flesh': take then thy bond, take thou thy pound of flesh, but in cutting it, if thou dost shed one drop of Christian blood, thy lands and goods are, by the laws of Venice, confiscate unto the state of Venice."

The knife faltered; the hand that held it shook and trembled and a dreadful bitterness curdled the Jew's fierce face. The very law he had invoked had defeated him. The mocking laughter of the court rang in his ears like the worst of Sunday's bells. He put away his knife; he rubbed and rubbed his hands, and muttered that he would take the offer of thrice the bond.

"Here is the money!" cried Bassanio, gladly.

But the small lawyer would not allow it; and, with a look of mingled affection and reproof at the extravagant young man, pressed Shylock still harder with the weight of the law. He was to have only what he had demanded, neither less nor more. Not even his principal was to be restored; only the pound of flesh without one drop of blood. He staggered, stared about him, saw only a sea of Christian faces and a sea of Christian smiles. He longed only to be gone. But even this was denied him. He, an alien, had undoubtedly sought the life of a citizen, therefore all his wealth was to be taken, half for the merchant, half for the state. His life itself was now in the hand of the Duke.

"Down therefore," cried the lawyer who had once urged him to show mercy, "and beg mercy of the Duke."

"That thou shall see the difference of our spirit," pronounced the Duke, "I pardon thee thy life before thou ask it . . ."

Shylock shook his head. He smiled bitterly. Of what use was his life now?

"Take my life and all," he whispered, "pardon not that. You take my house, when you do take the prop that doth sustain my house: you take my life when you do take the means whereby I live."

The small lawyer, who had, perhaps, been carried away by the ingeniousness of argument, was struck by the Jew's tragic words, and remembered. He turned to the merchant and asked:

"What mercy can you render him Antonio?"

Antonio proved no less merciful than the Duke. Half of Shylock's wealth should be restored, if he would, at his death, leave it to his daughter and her husband; the other half Antonio himself would use, and likewise bequeath to Jessica and Lorenzo. All this should be allowed upon one condition, that the Jew should turn Christian.

"Art thou contented Jew?" asked the lawyer, with the most gentle regard. "What dost thou say?"

"I am content," muttered the Jew; and, with bowed head, left the court to embrace a gentler God than the one that had brought him. As he went, the thronged candles tugged after him, as if to lend him a little of the radiance of a court in which, not justice, not the law, but mercy had triumphed.

When all were dispersed and the Duke departed, Bassanio embraced his saved friend; and together they thanked the small lawyer whose wit and skill had so marvellously succeeded. What gift could they give him? At first the lawyer would take nothing; but then, when pressed, asked no more than Bassanio's ring. Alas! it was the very ring that Portia had given him and which he'd sworn to keep so long as he should live. He made excuses, said it was not good enough, and offered, instead, to find the dearest ring in all Venice. But the lawyer would take nothing else, and so took nothing. Together with his small clerk, he left the court, making scornful comment upon those who offer and then turn niggardly when put to the performance.

"My lord Bassanio," urged Antonio, "let him have the ring . . ."

Bassanio sighed. He took the ring from his finger and sent Gratiano with it to overtake the small lawyer and his small clerk. So Bassanio parted with Portia's ring; and, at the same time, Gratiano parted with Nerissa's, for she, too, had given her husband a ring in love's pledge; which ring the lawyer's small clerk had begged.

The moon was high in Belmont and the dark gardens flowed with silver, like a Venice built in dreams.

"In such a night," sighed Lorenzo, as he strolled entwined with Jessica, and gave an instance of lovers long ago.

"In such a night," sighed Jessica, and gave another, no less apt.

"In such a night," proposed Lorenzo . . . and so they continued, night for night, until they were distracted by music that heralded the return of Portia and Nerissa, who were followed, soon after, by Bassanio and Gratiano, with the saved merchant Antonio, newly come from Venice. Lutes, guitars and viols sweet as honey swelled the tender meeting of wives and husbands . . . until a discord broke up the harmony. This discord concerned the giving of a ring. Gratiano, so it seemed, had given Nerissa's ring to a lawyer's clerk in Venice. Nerissa was outraged; and so was fair Portia when she learned that her husband, the ardent Bassanio, had given her ring to the lawyer. So much for love, so much for promises, so much for husbands' vows breathed in the first heat of passion! Antonio, much dismayed by the distress his own distress had brought about, sought to intercede. Portia sighed, and relented.

"Give him this," she sighed, "and bid him keep it better than the other." She gave the merchant a ring which he, in turn, gave to the apologising Bassanio. He took it, he glanced at it, he stared. It was the very ring he had given to the lawyer. Likewise, and at the same time, Gratiano was given the very ring he had bestowed upon the clerk. At once, base suspicions entered the minds of the husbands of how their wives might have come by the rings. But soon all was told, of how Portia had been the lawyer and Nerissa the clerk. So all ended in music, smiles and happiness; and fair Portia, practising the mercy she had preached, embraced her husband with all her heart.

Romeo and Juliet

In old Verona, where the streets were hot and narrow and the walls were high, where men were as bright as wasps and carried quick swords for their stings, there lived two families – the Capulets and the Montagues – who hated each other worse than death. They had but to pass in the street and they were at each other's throats like dogs in the sun. Cursing and shouting and bawling, and crashing from civil pillar to post, they filled the good people of Verona with fear and anger to have their city's peace so senselessly disturbed.

They were at it again! In the buzzing heat of a July morning, two lazy no-good servants of the Capulets had spied two strolling men of the Montagues. Looks had been exchanged, then words, and in moments the peaceful market was in an uproar as the four idle ruffians set about defending their masters' honour by smashing up stalls, overturning baskets, wrecking shops and wounding passers-by, in their valiant endeavours to cut each other into pieces.

Benvolio, a sensible young Montague, came upon the scene and tried to put a stop to it; Tybalt, a young Capulet so full of fury that he sweated knives, promptly went for Benvolio; old Montague and old Capulet appeared and tried to draw their doddering swords – that surely would have shaken more like straws in the wind than lightning in the sky. Men shouted, women screamed and rushed to drag wandering infants into safety ... and bloody riot threatened to swallow up all the fair city, till the Prince of Verona, with soldiers, came furiously into the square.

"Rebellious subjects, enemies to peace!" he roared; and, by dint of stern anger and sterner threats, restored some semblance of peace. The vile destructive brawling between the Montagues and the Capulets incensed him beyond measure.

"If ever you disturb our streets again," he swore, "your lives shall pay the forfeit."

When the Prince had gone, taking old Capulet with him, (to remove one half of the quarrel and so leave the other without an object), Lady Montague spoke to Benvolio.

"O where is Romeo, saw you him today?" she asked. "Right glad I am he was not at this fray," she added, as if Romeo, her only son, was as hot-headed as any and would surely have come to grief among the flashing swords and blundering fists. But Romeo had been elsewhere, wrapped in a melancholy that was most mysterious to his parents.

"See where he comes!" exclaimed Benvolio, as the young man in question drifted dolefully into the square, as if he was a ghost under instruction to haunt it. "So please you step aside," he urged old Montague and his wife, "I'll know his grievance . . ."

The parents departed, leaving Benvolio to penetrate the inscrutable mystery of his cousin Romeo's gloom. It proved no great task, as Romeo was all too willing to talk. He was in love. Hopelessly. He doted to distraction upon a glorious creature by the name of Rosalyne; and she would have nothing to do with him. So far as she was concerned, he was dust. Consequently he had been mooning all morning, lovesick, in a grove of sycamores.

Patiently Benvolio listened to the extensive cata-

78

logue of Rosalyne's amazing charms. He shook his head, and ventured to suggest that, if only Romeo looked about him, he might find others as fair. Impossible! The world was not so rich as to hold another such as Rosalyne. Benvolio expressed doubts, but Romeo was adamant; and so they continued, strolling through the golden warm streets of Verona, Romeo all melancholy passion and Benvolio all cheerful good sense.

"Why, Romeo, art thou mad?" began Benvolio when a servingman, much bewildered and with a paper in his hand, accosted them.

"I pray, sir, can you read?"

It seemed the fellow's master had entrusted him with a list of guests to be invited to a banquet that night. But, being no scholar, he could make neither head nor tail of the writing. Obligingly Romeo read out the names. They were a distinguished company – and among them was Rosalyne!

Where was the feast to be? Alas! at the house of old Capulet. A dangerous place for a Montague. But, if he went masked and in fantastical costume, as was the custom for uninvited guests at such a feast . . .

"Go thither," urged Benvolio, anxious to cure his cousin of that sickness called Rosalyne. He had noticed that on the list had been the best beauties of Verona, beside whom Rosalyne might well not shine so bright. "Compare her face," he advised shrewdly, "with some that I shall show; and I will make thee think thy swan a crow."

They met that night in the street outside the Capulet's house: Romeo, Benvolio and Mercutio, who was a kinsman of the Prince and Romeo's dearest friend. He was a lively, mocking youth, as full of bubbling laughter as a glass of good wine. They met by torchlight with some half dozen others, all in fantastical costume and gilded masks – as if King Midas had patted their heads and made fortunes of their faces.

Like gorgeous dragonflies, with partly folded wings, they leaned against the high wall that enclosed the Capulets' orchard, laughing and talking and trying, by all manner and means, to lift up Romeo's depressed spirits. But he, dressed as a rather splendid pilgrim, (in deference to the notion that any place that held Rosalyne must be a holy shrine), remained as dull as lead. Neither Benvolio's urging nor Mercutio's wit affected him. He stayed glum; and, furthermore, had had a strange premonition that the night's festivities would turn out to have been the beginning of a journey to the grave.

At length the maskers gave up their efforts and, with their gloomy companion, went into the feasting house. At once they were dazzled by a blaze of candles and a blaze of beauty . . . of silks and satins, soft white skin and dark, delighted eyes.

"You are welcome, gentlemen!" cried old Capulet, in holiday robes and cheerful to see so fine a company of maskers at his feast. "Come, musicians, play. A hall, a hall, give room! And foot it, girls!"

Music scraped and set a pulse, and the dancing began. Gowns rustled, filling the air with perfume; buckled shoes, like bright mice, twinkled in and out of richly swinging hems; fingers touched, hands entwined; masks and faces bobbed and turned, exchanging silver looks for golden smiles. All were dancing, but Romeo. He stood, marble pilgrim, stock-still and amazed! At last he spoke, to a servant standing by.

"What lady's that which doth enrich the hand of yonder knight?"

"I know not, sir," returned the servant.

"O she doth teach the torches to burn bright!" breathed Romeo, as he gazed at the girl whose beauty

had, in an instant, overturn
he had spoken softly, it had bee

"This by his voice should be a Mo

Tybalt had recognized the masker! He
that one of that hated name should dare to
Capulets' feast with his presence! He sent a pag
his rapier.

His uncle, old Capulet, sharply bade him keep his temper. It was a night of feast and revelry, and not to be spoiled. He command Tybalt to leave Romeo in peace.

"I'll not endure him!" cried Tybalt furiously.

"He shall be endured!" ordered old Capulet, with mounting indignation. "I say he shall. Go to, am I the master here or you? Go to!"

Unable to contain his anger, Tybalt departed. There was vengeance in his heart. He vowed that he would call Romeo to account for the supposed insult to the Capulets.

Romeo, unaware of the sudden hatred directed against him, moved among the dancers towards his sudden love. At last he stood before her and his eyes, inside his golden eyes, shone with rapture. Her loveliness had increased a hundredfold with nearness. Startled, she looked at the pilgrim and, such was the warmth of his passion, that she took fire herself.

Their hands touched; they spoke, half-humorously, half-solemnly. He begged a kiss. She was too young to hide her heart, and too innocent to pretend an innocence. She granted the request. Then, like children for the first time having tasted strawberries, they wanted more. They kissed again . . .

"Madam, your mother craves a word with you."

The world outside broke in upon them, in the shape of a female with a billowing bosom and skirts that might have covered half a country. Reluctantly the

...lgrim, and went in

...Romeo, following her
...ost among the throng.

...of the house," answered
...nurs'd her daughter that
...you," she confided, with a
...knowing smile that creased
...age bed, "he that can lay hold
...ninks."

...after her charge, leaving Romeo
dism... ...on of Montague, had fallen in love
with the ... ...of Capulet! Despairingly he cursed
the night in w...ch he had been so blessed, the night
when Romeo first set eyes on Juliet.

The maskers left the house and met outside, by the
orchard wall, meaning to make a night of it in
Verona's hot dark streets. Romeo was not among
them. They called him, searched for him, tried to
conjure him up in the name of his fair Rosalyne and
all her delicious parts. In vain. He did not appear; so
they went away, laughing loudly at the foolish melancholy of love.

Romeo heard them go. "He jests at scars," he
murmured, ruefully reflecting that, to him, love was
falling among roses and being savaged by their
thorns, "that never felt a wound."

He had climbed the high wall and was hiding in
shadows within the Capulets' orchard. His situation
was dangerous, but love lent a brightness to it, just
as danger lent an edge to his love. He gazed up
toward the dark side of the house. A light appeared
in a window, before which there was a balcony, like
a carved stone pocket some dozen feet from the
ground. The window opened and on to the balcony

stepped Juliet. She looked out on to the night, and sighed.

"O Romeo, Romeo, wherefore art thou Romeo?" she inquired most earnestly; and then, with gentle longing, urged: "Deny thy father and refuse thy name." She, like Romeo, had discovered that her greatest love was her father's greatest hate. She frowned and shook her head. "'Tis but they name that is my enemy," she argued with ingenious philosophy. "What's in a name? That which we call a rose by any other name would smell as sweet; so Romeo would, were he not Romeo call'd . . ."

So she continued, putting her case before an audience of moon and stars, until Romeo came from among the shadows and stood beneath the balcony. At once she was alarmed; then, when she saw who it was, was fearful for his safety in her father's garden; then ashamed when she realised that he must have overheard her private confession of love.

Eagerly Romeo dismissed the danger and rejoiced in the confession which, by its frankness, had short cut all tedious custom of roundabout approach and, in the twinkling of an eye, had plunged them both fathoms deep into each other's hearts, as if they had lived there all their lives. Even so, she begged him to leave as she feared more and more for his safety.

"O wilt thou leave me so unsatisfied?" pleaded Romeo.

"What satisfaction canst thou have tonight?" she answered gently.

"Th' exchange of thy love's faithful vow for mine!" he cried.

A voice called from within the room. It was Juliet's Nurse. Hurriedly Juliet begged Romeo to wait and went inside. A moment later she was back on the balcony.

"Three words, dear Romeo," she whispered down;

and then, scorning arithmetic, went on with many, many more. If Romeo was honourable, and his purpose marriage, she would send to him tomorrow so that he might tell her the time and place where the ceremony might be performed.

Again the Nurse called and again Juliet seemed plucked inside, as by an apron string; and again came back at once. More arrangements were made for the following day, and more love exchanged until, at last, there was no avoiding the parting.

"Good night, good night," sighed Juliet. "Parting is such sweet sorrow that I shall say good night till it be tomorrow."

She went back into her room. Romeo waited a little longer and then climbed back over the orchard wall. Rosalyne and all her charms had been swept from his mind and heart; and Juliet, too, had quite forgotten that she had been betrothed that very morning to a rich young man of her father's choice.

As soon as it was light, Romeo sought out his confessor, Friar Laurence, in a monastery some little way out of the town, and begged the worthy priest to marry him to Juliet that very day. At first the good Friar was too taken aback by the sudden setting of Rosalyne to comprehend the glorious sunrise of Juliet; but then, seeing the strength of Romeo's love, and knowing the honesty of his heart, and thinking that by such a union the hatred between the Montagues and the Capulets might be buried forever, he agreed to perform the ceremony. It was to take place in the holy Friar's cell on that afternoon. In high delight Romeo returned to the sunshine town to await Juliet's messenger.

While Romeo had been away from his house on his mission of love, Tybalt had called on a mission of hate. Not finding Romeo, he had left a letter, challenging the son of Montague to a duel to the death. This challenge had been found by Benvolio and Mercutio, who were still seeking their companion who had given them the slip on the previous night.

"Romeo will answer it," said Benvolio.

"Any man that can write may answer a letter," chuckled Mercutio; and the pair went their way through the bright streets, making fun of Tybalt and his fury.

Presently they met Romeo; but before they could tell him of the challenge, Juliet's Nurse, with skirts rolling and bosom billowing, came majestically down the street.

At once the three friends, overcome by the female's size and dignity, set about her like mad butterflies mocking an old cabbage. They twisted her, turned her, upended her words and her wits till she shook with indignation in all her bulging parts. At last she managed to say that it was Romeo she looked for, and Romeo alone; so Mercutio and Benvolio went away, laughing their heads off – and clean forgot about Tybalt and his murderous letter.

As soon as they were alone, the Nurse begged Romeo to deal honestly with Juliet, who was very young. Romeo swore he would.

"Bid her devise," he pleaded with the Nurse, "some means to come to shrift this afternoon. And there she shall at Friar Laurence' cell be shriv'd and married!"

Gleefully the Nurse received the news. Although she knew that Juliet was already betrothed to another, the prospect of a marriage and a wedding night acted upon her like strong wine. After all, so long as there was a husband, it mattered little whether it was one man or another. Full of thoughts of the bounding joys of the marriage bed, she rushed away to tell her young mistress and to prepare her.

That very afternoon, in Friar Laurence's cell,

Juliet and Romeo were married. Juliet became a Montague; and Romeo, in the same instant, became kin to all the Capulets. From the harsh soil of the two families' enmity, had sprung a single flower of love.

The day was hot and men's blood boiled in their veins. Tybalt, seeking a violent answer to his violent letter, came upon Romeo's two friends.

"Mercutio," he cried, with contempt in his voice and manner, "thou consortest with Romeo."

"Consort?" answered Mercutio angrily. "What, dost thou make us minstrels?"

Anxiously Benvolio tried to keep the peace that was so suddenly threatened. Romeo appeared. Tybalt turned aside from Mercutio.

"Well, peace be with you, sir," he said, "here comes my man." Coldly he insulted Romeo. Passers-by began to gather, but at a respectable distance; for surely there was going to be a fight. Tybalt challenged Romeo to draw his sword. Romeo refused. He had, within that hour, been married to Juliet and so was united with the house of Capulet. He would not, he could not shed any of their blood. But as the marriage was still secret, he was forced to hold his tongue.

"O calm, dishonourable, vile submission!' cried Mercutio, unable to understand Romeo's reluctance to fight. "Tybalt, you rat-catcher, will you walk?"

He drew his sword and, in a moment, he and mad Tybalt were thrusting and parrying and darting at each other with their shining deadly strings.

"Draw, Benvolio," cried Romeo, aghast. "Beat down their weapons. Gentlemen, for shame, forbear this outrage. Tybalt, Mercutio!"

He seized his friend, meaning to hold him back. Murderous Tybalt lunged; and his sword, like a thin snake, struck under Romeo's arm and pierced Mercutio's breast. Then he fled.

"I am hurt," muttered Tybalt, finding himself to be a sudden victim of the hatred between Capulet and Montague. "A plague o' both your houses."

"What, art thou hurt?" asked Benvolio, supporting Mercutio, who was sinking to the ground.

"Ay, ay, a scratch, a scratch . . ."

"Courage, man," urged Romeo, "the hurt cannot be much."

"No, 'tis not so deep as a well," agreed Mercutio, "nor so wide as a church door, but 'tis enough, 'twill serve. Ask for me tomorrow, and you shall find me a grave man. I am peppered, I warrant, for this world. A plague o' both your houses . . ."

He was carried into the nearest house and soon after, the news came out that Mercutio, brave, witty, laughing Mercutio, was dead. Even as Romeo stood, amazed and overcome with grief, and blaming himself for his friend's death, Tybalt returned.

This time Romeo did not refuse the challenge. He drew his sword, and, mad for revenge, beat down Tybalt's furious blade – which was still red with Mercutio's blood – and killed him before he knew what he had done.

"Romeo!" cried Benvolio, terrified by the sudden disaster. "Away, be gone . . .! The Prince will doom thee death if thou art taken. Hence, be gone, away!"

Only then did Romeo understand. On the very day he had married, he had killed his new wife's kinsman and so condemned himself to death.

"O I am fortune's fool!" he wept, and rushed away; leaving Tybalt spidered on the ground and slowly reddening Verona's street.

He fled for sanctuary to Friar Laurence's cell and there, shaking and trembling, he learned that the

Prince had been merciful. As the quarrel had been forced upon Romeo, the Prince had sentenced him to banishment instead of to death. He was to leave Verona and never set foot inside its walls again. Such was the Prince's mercy, but to Romeo it was worse than death. Not to see Juliet again was to condemn him to a living grave. The good Friar tried to reason with him, to teach him to make the best of the life that had been granted.

"Thou canst not speak of that thou dost not feel!" cried Romeo in despair. "Wert thou as young as I, Juliet thy love, an hour but married, Tybalt murdered, doting like me, and like me banished, then mightst thou speak . . ."

To this there was no answer; for who could know what Romeo felt but Romeo, and who could know that Juliet was his world? Had he been older, he might have been wiser . . . if indeed it's wisdom to be calculating in affection and circumspect in love.

There was a knock upon the door. It was the Nurse, come in haste from her mistress, who was in despair over the death of her dear cousin and the banishment of her husband. Romeo's remorse knew no bounds. He threatened to kill himself; but the holy Friary stayed his hand.

"Go," he advised the wildly grieving youth, "get thee to thy love as was decreed. Ascend her chamber – hence, and comfort her."

Hope revived as Romeo listened to the Friar's words. He would spend that night – his wedding night – in Juliet's arms; and early on the following day, he would go to Mantua where he would wait until his marriage might be made known and the Prince's pardon obtained. The Friar would send to him . . .

* * *

The orchard was dark, but the stars were pale. Presently a bird began to sing. The new husband and the new wife, sleepy from love, came out on to the balcony, which held them like another bed, a bed of stone.

"It is not yet near day," lied Juliet. "It was the nightingale and not the lark . . ."

Romeo shook his head. "It was the lark, the herald of the morn . . . Look, love . . . night's candles are burnt out."

"Yond light is not daylight," denied Juliet. "I know it . . ."

But it was to no avail. The night was over and the time for parting come.

"Farewell, farewell, one kiss and I'll descend," murmured Romeo. They embraced, and he slipped unwillingly from Juliet's despairing arms, and climbed down to the dark ground. He looked up and she, overhanging the balcony, with her willow hair weeping, stared down; and each, in that last moment, was chilled with a sudden foreboding and seemed to see the other pale and dead. Then Romeo was gone.

The Capulet's house was in sad confusion. Tybalt had been laid to rest and Juliet, supposedly grieving for her murdered cousin, was a ghost of sobs and tears. Old Capulet, ever impatient with the sorrows of the young – which, to him, were as trifling as the peevish mewing of a baby, to be quietened by a sweet or a new toy – spoke with his wife and the County Paris, the excellent and well-connected youth to whom he had betrothed his daughter.

"What day is this?" he demanded.

"Monday, my lord," said Paris.

"Monday! Ha, ha! Well, Wednesday is too soon. A Thursday let it be, a Thursday, tell her," he instructed his wife, "she shall be married to this noble earl." He nodded with high satisfaction. A husband was the very thing to quieten his wailing child. "We'll have some half a dozen friends," he decided, "and there an end. But what say you to Thursday?"

The youth was in agreement and old Capulet was satisfied that the joyful tidings of such an occasion would put a stop to his daughter's grief.

The joyful tidings were received; but far from joyfully. Juliet was filled with dread and horror. Too frightened to confess that she was already married, and to a Montague, she sought frantically to avoid, to delay this impossible second marriage.

"Here comes your father," said Lady Capulet, shocked by her daughter's reluctance to obey her parents' command. "Tell him so yourself and see how he will take it at your hands."

The father was no better pleased. Turning in fury on his disobedient child, he shouted: "But fettle your fine joints 'gainst Thursday next to go with Paris to Saint Peter's Church, or I will drag thee on a hurdle thither. Out, you green-sickness carrion! Out, you baggage! You tallow-face!"

"Good father!" pleaded Juliet, weeping and on her knees.

"Hang thee young baggage!" raged her father. "Get thee to church a Thursday or never after look me in the face!"

Then, when the father and mother had gone, the Nurse took up their cause, but more gently.

"I think it best you married with the County," she urged; for a second marriage meant no more to her than another joyful, bounding wedding night. "O he's a lovely gentleman," she sighed. "Romeo's a dishclout to him . . ."

"Well, thou hast comforted me marvellous much," said Juliet, her last prop gone and with nothing left in all the world to cling to but Romeo's love. "Go in and tell my lady I am gone, having displeas'd my father, to Laurence' cell, to make confession and to be absolv'd."

To the monastery she went, and there, in the holy Friar's cell, poured out all her misery and despair. The old man listened and, moved by Juliet's all-consuming love for Romeo, and also concerned for the sin he would be bringing upon himself by performing a second marriage, devised a strange, fantastic plan. If this plan succeeded, then great happiness would be the result. If it failed, then Verona, Juliet and Romeo, Capulet and Montague, would stand for ever in the world's memory for love's tragedy.

This was the Friar's plan. He knew of a liquor that, if drunk, would produce so exact a counterfeit of death that none could tell the difference. This state would continue for two and forty hours, after which there would be a harmless awakening. On the Wednesday night, when she was alone, Juliet was to drink this liquor so that, when her people came to wake her in the morning for her wedding, they would find her seeming dead. Then, as was the custom, she would be laid in her best attire in the family monument. There, after a proper time, she would awaken and Romeo would be beside her. Letters would have been sent to Mantua telling him of the plan, so that he and Juliet might escape together to safety and happiness.

"I'll send a friar with speed," promised the old priest.

"Love give me strength," prayed Juliet, taking the vial of liquor from Friar Laurence. "Farewell, dear father."

In darkly winding Mantua, news came to Romeo from Verona. But not from Friar Laurence. It was news brought by Romeo's servant; and it was as black as hell. Juliet was dead.

"Leave me," muttered Romeo, sick with amazement and grief. "Hast thou no letters to me from the Friar?"

There was none; for what more could be told than that Romeo's world was lost and his life was a vain pretence? He went to buy strong poison from an apothecary; and set off for Verona and Juliet's tomb.

"Well, Juliet," he whispered, "I will lie with thee tonight."

The letter telling Romeo the truth of what had happened had never left Verona. The wretched brother who had been entrusted with it had been shut up in a house suspected of the plague, and it was night before he was freed.

He went at once to Friar Laurence and told him of the misadventure. The Friar was filled with deep concern. Juliet would soon awaken and she would be alone in a dead man's tomb. He himself must go to the monument and be on hand for the awakening.

The churchyard was dark and the yew trees stood black among the pale monuments, as if the day's mourners had left their shadows behind. Paris, the unlucky bridegroom who, on his wedding morning had come to claim his bride and found her dead, now came with tears and flowers to her midnight tomb. He sent his page a little way off, to warn him of any intruder, for he wanted to mourn and weep in solitude.

Presently the page whistled. Someone was approaching. Paris hid from sight. The intruder appeared. It was that Montague who had been banished for murdering poor Juliet's cousin. What further act of violence was he about to commit? Dear God! He was opening sweet Juliet's tomb!

"Stop thy unhallowed toil, vile Montague!" he cried. "Can vengeance be pursued further than death?"

Romeo turned. His face was pale, as if death had already touched it. He begged Paris leave him and be gone. Enraged, Paris tried to seize him for a felon.

"Wilt thou provoke me?" shouted Romeo. "Then have at thee, boy!"

They drew their swords, and there, among the solemn dead, they fought like madmen; until one, young Paris, fell dying to the ground.

"If thou be merciful," he begged his unwilling murderer, "open the tomb, lay me with Juliet."

"In faith I will," promised Romeo, but to a man already dead.

He dragged him into the monument and laid him down within the low, vaulted chamber where, among stored-up Capulets, long-since ransacked by worms, lay Juliet upon a bed of stone. Death had not yet begun to spoil her; she might be living still. He knelt beside her and made his sad farewell.

"Eyes, look your last. Arms, take your last embrace! And lips, O you the doors of breath, seal with a righteous kiss a dateless bargain to engrossing Death." Then, with a sudden joyfulness he cried. "Here's to my love!" and drank the apothecary's poison; and so, in an instant, ended for ever the parting from his love.

When Friar Laurence, old, hobbling, infirm and fearful, at last entered the tomb, Romeo was dead; and Juliet just awakening.

"O comfortable Friar, where is my lord?" she asked gently. "Where is my Romeo?"

Wretchedly he told her; and wretchedly begged her to come away.

"Go, get thee hence," she answered, with a dignity that would have humbled a king, "for I will not away."

The old priest, who had meant so well and done so

ill, crept away from the consequence of his endeavours; and left Juliet alone with her dead.

Longingly she kissed Romeo's lips in the hope that some poison still remained on them. There was none; so she took his dagger and pressed it lovingly into her heart.

So, in old Verona, died Juliet and Romeo, who loved at last sight no less than at their first. The fathers – old Capulet and Montague – were grief-stricken by the tragic deaths of their children, and ashamed that their old hate had brought it about. They vowed eternal friendship to one another; and now the Capulets and Montagues, and old Verona, live only in the great love of Juliet and Romeo.

A Midsummer Night's Dream

Hermia, who was small, dark and perfect, loved Lysander; and Lysander loved Hermia. What could have been better than that? At the same time, Helena, who was tall, fair and tearful, loved Demetrius.

But Demetrius did not love Helena. Instead he, too, loved Hermia . . . who did not love him. What could have been worse than that?

Now although Lysander and Demetrius were both young, handsome and rich, so that, to the untouched heart and the uncomplicated eye, there was nothing to choose between them, Hermia's father had made a choice. He had chosen Demetrius; and such was the harsh law of Athens, where they all lived, that Hermia had to obey her father and marry Demetrius, or be shut up in a nunnery for the rest of her life.

So Hermia was in despair, Lysander was in torment, Demetrius was triumphant, and Helena, loving and unloved, wept like a willow over a stream of her own making. It was a pitiable state of affairs, and it could not have been better put than by Lysander, who declared that:

"The course of true love never did run smooth."

But nonetheless, run it did, on eager, fearful feet, to a certain wood not far from the town. There, in the moon washed time of night, Lysander and Hermia planned to meet and fly to some distant place where they would be safe from the cruel Athenian law.

95

All would have been well had not Hermia, warm-hearted, confiding Hermia, told Helena, who was her longest, dearest friend. Helena, more doleful than ever, and hoping for no more than a glance of gratitude and a rag of his company, played the tell-tale and told Demetrius of the flight. Demetrius was outraged. He rushed off to the wood, meaning to win Hermia's heart by plunging his sword into Lysander's. And after him went Helena, in despairing pursuit.

Nor were these love-tangled four the only ones who went to the wood upon that Midsummer's night; for no man, not even a lover, can have the world to himself. Six good men and true, six solid workmen of Athens, engaged to meet there in secret. They were to rehearse a play for the festivities of Duke Theseus's marriage to Hippolyta, once his enemy but soon to be his love.

Very serious was their business, for if their play was chosen, they would all be given pensions and stand high in the esteem of their fellow workmen in the town. The play, as was right for a wedding, was of lovers; so the six good men and true, with their heads full of passions and pensions, went to the wood, where already, in thicket and clearing, there was love in earnest and love in despair.

It was a strange wood, as huge, dark and mysterious as a man's mind. It was haunted – and by more than spinning spiders, beetles, hedgehogs and softly gliding, spotted snakes. There were other personages who flickered among the shadows, darted across moonbeams, hung in the beating air and pursued mysterious affairs of their own.

"Ill met by moonlight, proud Titania!"

Oberon, dread King of the night! Shadowy, formidable, with train of goblins, sprites and elves; and with Puck, his grinning, mocking henchman by his side; stepped suddenly into the moonshine and stood, a dark threat in a silver world.

Over and against him, caught in brightness with delicate foot unplaced, Titania, his queen, drew back with hands upraised in anger.

"What, jealous Oberon? Fairies, skip hence! I have forsworn his bed and company!"

Strange quarrel between these powerful rulers of the night time world! Titania had as her attendant a changeling Indian boy that Oberon desired for himself. But Oberon's request had been denied, and his command scorned. So there was discord in the world of spirits no less than in the world of men. In consequence, the very seasons had been disturbed: killing frosts and drowning floods had spoiled the spring and bewildered the summer, for a quarrel between so dangerous a King and so wild a Queen, made a sickness in Nature herself.

"Do you amend it then; it lies in you," accused Oberon. "I do but beg a little changeling boy . . ."

"Not for thy fairy kingdom!" vowed Titania. And, with her gossamer train attending, swept from the glade, leaving her shadowy lord to brood angrily on his disappointment.

"Well, go thy way," he murmured at length. "Thou shalt not from this grove till I torment thee for this injury."

Presently the notion of a strange revenge came into his ranging thoughts. There was, he knew, a certain purple flower that grew, far, far away in the west, that was possessed of an uncanny power. If the juice of this flower was dropped upon sleeping eyelids, then the sleeper, on awakening, would fall wildly, madly in love with the very next living creature – be it lion, bear, wolf or monkey, no matter how vile – that the magically anointed eyes beheld.

"Fetch me this herb," commanded Oberon to Puck,

his lurking henchman, "and be thou here again ere the leviathan can swim a league."

"I'll put a girdle round about the earth," promised Puck, a prick-eared child with a crooked grin, whose chief delight was fright and confusion, "in forty minutes!" And off he sped, like a wicked arrow, from his dread master's side.

Lost in thought, the King awaited his servant's return until suddenly, the murmuring quiet of the wood was disturbed. There came a violent crashing, and rending, and gasping, and panting, as of wild beasts lost and confused. At once the brooding King drew the night about him, like a cloak, and became no more than the shadow of a shadow . . .

The commotion burst out into the pooled moonlight and made it shake.

"I love thee not, therefore pursue me not!" It was the furious Demetrius with Helena wailing hopelessly in his wake. "Hence, get thee gone and follow me no more!"

Her tale-bearing had done her no good. Instead of her lover's company, she'd gained only the sight of his avoiding back; and instead of his gratitude, she'd had only his shoulder-flung abuse. But still she pursued him, weeping and sobbing her love.

"I am your spaniel," she wailed; "and, Demetrius, the more you beat me, I will fawn on you. Use me but as your spaniel," she pleaded. "Only give me leave, unworthy as I am, to follow you!"

"I am sick when I do look on thee!" shouted Demetrius, feeling unwanted love at his heels like a stone in his shoe.

"And I am sick when I look not on you!" sobbed Helena.

"Let me go!" cried Demetrius, wild only to find Hermia and kill Lysander. "Or if thou follow me do not believe but I shall do thee mischief in the wood!"

But Helena was past caring. So far gone was she in love that custom, modesty, and maidenly restraint were but as specks on the horizon, and remembered only with a pang.

"We should be woo'd," she wept, "and were not made to woo!"

Demetrius escaped, and Helena, with a doleful cry, plunged after. The glade stood empty of all save moonlight and the memory of distress. Then Oberon became visible, as if in the thinning of a mist.

"Fare thee well, nymph," he murmured, gazing after the broken-hearted lady. "Ere he do leave this grove, thou shalt fly him, and he shall seek thy love."

As he stood meditating on how this reversal might be brought about, Puck returned breathlessly to his side, holding out the little purple flower. Oberon's eyes glittered mysteriously as he took it.

"I know a bank where the wild thyme blows," he whispered, as his fancy brought it before his mind's eye. "There sleeps Titania some time of the night." Dreamily he crushed the flower between his pale fingers so that its liquor ran into a cup, held out by the eager Puck. "And with the juice of this I'll streak her eyes, and make her full of hateful fantasies . . ."

He smiled vengefully; and then, remembering the distress that had passed so recently before his invisible eyes, he bade Puck take a little of the juice and anoint the eyes of the scornful youth so that, when he waked, he should dote to distraction on the tall, fair, tearful lady who had so unavailingly pursued him.

"Thou shalt know the man," he instructed, "by the Athenian garments he hath on."

"Fear not, my lord," assured Puck; "your servant shall do so."

* * *

Now the wood was quiet, and folded in night; and the moon's dream self drifted, among mirrored branches, in stream and pool. The two wanderers, dark master and quick servant, crept among the shadowy trees, each with his portion of the charmed liquor: the one to make love run mad, the other to make love run smooth and prosperous to life's end.

First Oberon found what he sought, and while Titania slumbered, and her drowsy sentinels nodded at their posts, he streaked her sleeping eyes with the purple flower's juice.

"What thou seest when thou dost wake," he breathed; "do it for thy true love take . . . Wake when some vile thing is near."

He left her sleeping and so cloaked and canopied in the garments of nature that the youth and the girl who came into the glade soon after saw nothing but leaves and flowers. But then they never looked to see a sleeping queen, for they had eyes only for each other.

Hermia and Lysander, those dear lovers in perfect accord, were weary from walking, and were lost.

"We'll rest us, Hermia," proposed Lysander, "if you think it good."

"Be it so, Lysander," agreed small, dark Hermia, with a downward cast of her eyes; "find you out a bed, for I upon this bank will rest my head."

"One turf shall serve as pillow for us both," said Lysander, with a tenderness that filled sweet Hermia with grave misgivings.

"Nay, good Lysander; for my sake, my dear, lie further off yet; do not lie so near."

Fervently Lysander protested that his intentions were most honourable and urged his lovely Hermia to reconsider her unkind decision. But Hermia shook her head.

"Lie further off, in human modesty," she insisted

100

with gentle reproach. "Such separation as may well be said becomes a virtuous bachelor and a maid. So far be distant; and good night, sweet friend."

Lysander sighed but, deferring to his lady, found himself a bed some little way removed; and presently the lovers, united in spirit though divided in flesh, closed their eyes in sleep.

So they lay when Puck found them and, surprised and vexed to see so much distance between them, instantly took them for the youth and girl he had been told to find.

"This is he my master said despised the Athenian maid . . . and here the maiden sleeping sound, on the dank and dirty ground!" the goblin cried indignantly. "Pretty soul! she durst not lie near this lack-love, this kill-courtesy!"

Straightway and without another thought, he anointed Lysander's closed eyes with the charmed juice, and returned to Oberon, well pleased with his success.

No sooner had he departed than calamity came into the glade. It came with a rush and a cry and a moan and a wail. It came in the shape of doleful Helena. Chivvied by bush and fingered by briar, with her gown in as many tatters and shreds as her heart, she paused, panting for breath. She had lost Demetrius and knew not where to turn.

"But who is here?" she cried. "Lysander on the ground?"

She rushed and knelt beside him, hanging her anxious face above his, like a sad moon with lips, eyes and streaming silken hair. "Lysander, if you live, good sir, awake!"

He awoke, opened his betwitched eyes, saw Helena (for there was little else within his scope!) and loved her madly, as he had never loved before!

Shocked beyond measure, Helena drew back, reminded Lysander that it was Hermia he loved –

"Not Hermia but Helena I love," cried Lysander. "Who will not change a raven for a dove?" And he poured out so wild a torrent of passion that Helena quailed before it and thought herself to be most unkindly mocked.

"O that a lady of one man refused," she sobbed, "should of another therefore be abused!" And she fled from the clearing, dismayed.

Lysander, seeing the sleeping Hermia, wondered how he could ever have loved her.

"Hermia," he cried – but softly for he did not want to awaken her, "sleep thou there, and never mayest thou come Lysander near!"

Then off he rushed in pursuit of Helena, who pursued Demetrius, who in his turn, pursued Hermia, who laying sleeping and abandoned, with nothing for company but troubled dreams.

She awoke and called out for Lysander. There was no answer. She looked: the glade was empty. She called again:

"Lysander! lord! What, out of hearing? Gone? No sound, no word?"

She trembled, she shook, she cried out in terror; and then, like Helena before her, fled from the clearing, dismayed!

The glade was still and the troubled moonlight calm again; so that the disturbed bushes and shaken leaves were restored to skilful silverware. Oberon's queen still slept upon her secret couch; her magically anointed eyes had yet to open . . .

"Are we all met?" came a plain, sturdy voice.

"Pat, pat," came another; "and here's a marvellous convenient place for our rehearsal."

The six good men and true, the six worthy work-

102

men of Athens, clumped into the moonlight glade, paused and peered thoughtfully about them.

"This green plot shall be our stage," decided Peter Quince, a carpenter by trade. He was the most scholarly of the company and was to produce the play.

The parts had been given out and all was now to go forward, exactly as it would be before the Duke. That is, if their play was chosen.

"Peter Quince!"

Nick Bottom, the weaver, spoke up, and everybody paid attention. Among every company of men there is always one to be reckoned with, one that it is good to have on your side, one whose abilities mark him out as a mine of intellect and a tower of strength.

Such a man was Bottom the weaver: large, big-faced and with little eyes ringed round with red, as if to emphasize their importance. He was down for Pyramus in the play, which was the lover's part and the most important; for none but Bottom could have undertaken it. He might have playcd Thisbe, the lady, with equal success; he might have played the Lion, who frightened poor Thisbe away; he might have played any or all of the other parts – for he had a genius for each of them, as everyone agreed – but he had to play Pyramus, for none but Bottom could have undertaken it. Without Bottom there could be no Pyramus; and without Pyramus there could be no play. The whole enterprise was founded on Bottom; and without a Bottom it would have fallen through.

"Peter Quince!"

"What sayest thou, bully Bottom?"

Bottom had a great deal to say, and all of it good sturdy sense. He had discovered that Pyramus, in the play, was to kill himself, which would distress the ladies in their audience to such an extent that the hoped-for pensions might well be in peril. Everyone

103

nodded wisely and looked to Bottom for a solution. They were not disappointed.

"Write me a prologue," said Bottom, "to say we will do no harm with our swords, and that Pyramus is not killed indeed. Tell them that I, Pyramus, am not Pyramus, but Bottom the weaver. This will put them out of fear."

He smiled, and everyone looked relieved. Truly was Bottom a man of infinite resource, and a very present help in time of need.

So the rehearsal went forward, with tireless assistance from Bottom, who was never at a loss to improve the play. With all solemnity the six good men and true transformed themselves into ardent lovers, a ravening lion and a patient wall (for a wall was required and there was none nearby); and Peter Quince, with book in hand, sometimes admiring, sometimes critical, guided the progress of the play.

But Peter Quince was not the only auditor; or, for that matter, the only critic of the proceedings.

"What hempen homespuns have we swaggering here, so near the cradle of the Fairy Queen?"

Puck, lurking among leaves, peered out at the worthy workmen's solemn antics. He grinned crookedly, and his eyes glittered like spots of dew.

"I'll meet thee, Pyramus, at Ninny's tomb," announced Francis Flute, the bellows-mender, who, though he had a beard coming, and was bashful about it, played the lady Thisbe.

"Ninus' tomb, man!" cried Peter Quince, crossly. "Why you must not speak that yet; that you answer to Pyramus." Then, losing patience with Flute, who, though earnest, was slow of learning, accused him bitterly: "You speak all your part at once, cues and all." He shook his head and sighed. Come what would to try him, the play must go on. "Pyramus, enter!" he called. "Your cue is past . . ."

Bottom, who had retired within a hawthorn brake, stepped forth with that mixture of modesty and expectation that marks the well-graced actor who knows that all eyes will be upon him, and the rest of the company ignored. His expectations were answered. All eyes were most certainly upon him – and to a bulging extent.

His companions stared, glared, shook, trembled, turned white, turned grey . . . and most precipitantly fled! Bottom, surprised, could make nothing of it. He shook his head. Peter Quince returned, briefly and timorously. He stared at Bottom, appalled.

"Bless thee, Bottom, bless thee! Thou art translated."

Then he retired again in melancholy terror. Bottom frowned and looked down upon himself to see what cause there was for dismay. None. There were his own stout arms, his own good stomach, his own sturdy legs that ended up, as might have been expected, in his own large, familiar boots. All that he could see was as it should have been, and proper to Bottom. It was only what he saw with that was not. From the neck down he was Bottom the weaver; from the neck up he was – a monster!

While he had waited in the hawthorn brake, listening for his cue, Puck had touched his broad brow and made it harsh and hairy, had touched his nose and made it a muzzle, and had touched his ears and made them grow. In short, he had clapped upon the shoulders of the unsuspecting Bottom, the sickening head of an ass!

"I see their knavery," said Bottom, by way of a dignified reproof to his departed companions; "this is to make an ass of me . . ." He walked up and down and began to sing in a loud voice to keep up his spirits. He was divided between mystification and anger over the behaviour of his friends; for he, no more than any man, could see that he had a donkey's head.

Puck watched with rare delight, and guided the weaver's steps nearer and nearer to the bed of the Fairy Queen. Suddenly she awoke, and opened her anointed eyes.

"What angel wakes me from my flowery bed?" she cried, hearing Bottom's braying voice and then seeing him in all his hairy, long-eared glory.

Bottom acknowledged the greeting of the Fairy Queen, and then continued with his song, for he was not a man easily amazed.

"I pray thee, gentle mortal, sing again!" begged Titania; and, helpless with admiration, confessed to the donkey-headed Bottom that she loved him at first sight.

"Methinks, mistress, you should have little reason for that," said Bottom in all honesty; and went on to express a wish to find his way out of the wood. But that was not to be.

"Thou shalt remain here," commanded Titania, "whether thou wilt or no. I am a spirit of no common rate," she declared, rising from her couch in all her strange beauty and majesty. "And I do love thee; therefore go with me."

Bottom bowed his long-eared head in courteous assent, and bright Titania awarded him four gossamer sprites to tend upon him and supply his every want. So Bottom, whom nothing could surprise – for, though he had an ass's head, he had a rare soul – went affably with the Fairy Queen, while the four sprites waited on his smallest command. He bore himself like a monarch . . .

These matters Puck reported to his master, who nodded, well-pleased by the grotesque punishment that had been visited on his disobedient Queen.

"But hast thou," he asked, "yet latch'd the Athenian's eyes with the love-juice, as I did bid thee do?"

"I took him sleeping," promised Puck, "that is finish'd, too." Even as he said it, Demetrius and Hermia came into the glade.

"Stand close;" murmured Oberon, dissolving into a kind of mist, "this is the same Athenian."

"This is the woman," agreed Puck, thinning by his master's side; "but not this the man."

Puck had blundered. Demetrius still loved Hermia, who still loved Lysander, who now, by reason of Puck's mistake, loved Helena who, therefore, must still love where she was despised.

"See me no more!" cried small dark Hermia, wearied and distressed by the unwanted Demetrius. And she plunged away in pursuit of her lost Lysander. Demetrius gazed after her in despair.

"There's no following her in this fierce vein," he sighed regretfully; and, overcome with weariness from the chase, lay down to rest.

"What hast thou done?" demanded Oberon, vexed by his servant's error. "About the wood go swifter than the wind, and Helena of Athens look thou find!"

The goblin vanished and Oberon softly approached the sleeping Demetrius.

"When his love he doth espy, let her shine," he whispered, anointing the sleeper's eyes with the liquor of the purple flower. "When thou wak'st, if she be by, beg of her for remedy."

Even as this was done Puck returned, leading in his invisible wake the melancholy Helena who, in her turn, was followed by the eye-bewitched Lysander. Demetrius awoke, opened his charmed eyes, saw Helena and straightway fell madly, wildly in love with her! No sooner had he declared himself, than Hermia returned and there followed a scene of such frantic confusion, such anger, such reproach, such

107

accusation and denial, such brandishing of fists and flashing of eyes, such wounding with words and breaking of hearts, that, had there been mortal eyes to watch, they would have made a waterfall of tears, instead of glinting with merriment at love's calamity.

"Lord what fools these mortals be!" chuckled Puck, as the four lovers raved and ranted and wept in the moonlit glade.

"You juggler! You canker-blossom!" shouted Hermia, maddened by the very sight of Helena, once without a lover and now the undeserving possessor of two. "You thief of love!"

"Have you no modesty, no maiden shame?" wondered Helena, tottering like a stricken willow before the injustice of Hermia's reproach. "You puppet, you!"

"Puppet?" shrieked Hermia, mortified by so unkind a reference to her brevity of inches. "Thou painted maypole!"

"Let her not hurt me!" screeched Helena, skipping, like a timid doe, behind Demetrius and Lysander, as Hermia flew at her with upraised nails. "She was a vixen when she went to school!"

The quarrel leaped and blazed. Spiders, beetles, serpents and distracted birds fled from the heated scene; and the passions of the four lovers could no longer be confined within the pressing limits of the glade. Demetrius and Lysander, unable to endure each other's existence for an instant more, reached for their swords and rushed away in search of plainer ground where they might make fountains with each other's blood.

The two ladies thus abandoned in the moonlight, and panting from their recent exertions, eyed each other with strong dislike and deep distrust. Then first one, and then the other, retreated and vanished into darkness, to seek kindness and security among the less wild beasts that might inhabit the wood.

* * *

108

"This is thy negligence," accused Oberon, coming out from leaves and regarding his henchman with disfavour. "Still thou mistak'st, or else committ'st thy knaveries wilfully."

"Believe me, king of shadows, I mistook," protested Puck, whose goblin heart had, nonetheless, been gladdened by the sight of the crossed and crossing lovers. The four-fold enmity that had sprung from a single misplaced love had furnished him with much salty delight.

But now it was to be ended. Oberon commanded Puck to prevent the coming battle between Lysander and Demetrius, and then to undo the harm that magic had done with magic again. While Puck was so employed he would find the donkey-doting Titania and gain his chief object which was to take her Indian boy.

"Up and down, up and down," cried Puck, who foresaw as much confusion in undoing confusion as in making it, "I will lead them up and down!"

Away he sped into the wood where first he found Lysander, baffled by thicket, ditch and moonshine, shouting for his enemy and waving his sword wherever there was space to do so.

"Where art thou, proud Demetrius?"

"Here, villain, drawn and ready!" answered Puck, in Demetrius's voice.

"I'll be with thee straight!" swore Lysander and went off as round-about as Puck could lead him, fighting with bushes, branches and shadows every step of the way.

Next he taunted Demetrius with Lysander's voice; then back to Lysander, then Demetrius again, then with goblin speed, to furious Lysander. He was here, he was there, he was in front, he was behind, he was everywhere, he was nowhere!

"Follow my voice!" he called; and follow it the

maddened lovers did, until the wood was filled with shouts and cries and grunts and gasps, and the glitter of swords as they slashed at moonbeams and pierced the dark. Then, little by little, the passionate enemies grew slower in their motions. Their limbs ached and their bright swords, no longer flashing, helped them, like sticks or crutches, on their weary way. At length first one and then the other tottered into the very glade from which they'd set out; and, unaware of each other, thankfully lay down and went to sleep.

"O weary night, O long and tedious night!" wailed Helena, straying upon the scene and seeing nothing but her own sadness. Her heart was broken. She sighed and sank down upon the grass and prayed for sleep.

"Yet but three?" cried Puck, examining with interest the unconscious contents of the glade. "Come one more, two of both kinds makes up four!"

"I can no further crawl, no further go;" sobbed Hermia, shredded alike by misery and briar. "Here will I rest me till the break of day!"

And she joined the three sleepers to make up the goblin's four.

"Sleep sound!" whispered Puck and, darting forward, squeezed the fateful juice into Lysander's dreaming eyes. "When thou wak'st," he promised, "thou tak'st true delight in the sight of thy former lady's eye!"

He vanished, leaving the four strewn upon the grass, like fallen warriors on love's battlefield.

"Come sit thee down upon this flowery bed," begged the Fairy Queen, marvellous in the moonlight, "while I thy amiable cheeks do coy . . . and kiss thy fair large ears . . ."

Bottom, sturdy, donkey-headed Bottom, brayed

110

with pleasure and with dignity, submitted himself to Titania's embrace.

Crowned and wreathed and stuck all over with admiring roses, Bottom laid himself down upon Titania's couch, while his attendant sprites scratched him and tickled him and supplied his every want. Presently, the weariness of endlessly fulfilled desires overcame him.

"I have," he declared with a yawn, "an exposition of sleep come upon me."

"Sleep thou," murmured the Fairy Queen. "O how I love thee! How I dote on thee!"

So Bottom slumbered, and his loud snores made a thunderous lullaby that soon lulled Titania and her court into sleep! Sleep! The glade was filled with it, and the very moonlight seemed to dream. Bushes nodded and flowers turned and dozed, as Oberon and his henchman came softly among them. The kind of shadows, having obtained the Indian boy, looked down with pity on his bewitched queen.

"I will undo this hateful imperfection of her eyes," he whispered; and doing so, with the juice of another herb, bade Titania wake.

"My Oberon!" she cried, "What visions have I seen! Methought I was enamoured of an ass!"

"There lies your love," said Oberon; and Titania gazed appalled upon the vision of flowery, snoring, donkey-headed Bottom.

"How came these things to pass?" she demanded; but Oberon smiled and shook his head. Then, bidding Puck restore Bottom to his human state, he took Titania by the hand and led her, dancing, from the sleeping scene.

The sounds of hounds and horn came winding through the wood. Duke Theseus and his future queen were out upon the morning's hunt.

Presently the Royal riders entered the glade and gazed down in wonderment upon the sleepers.

"My lord, this is my daughter here asleep!" cried Hermia's father, who was of the company. Seeing how things were, he demanded that the full rigour of the law should be visited directly on his truant child.

But when the lovers were awakened, all could see that, either by magic, witchcraft, or merely by true love finding out true heart (which must be magical enough!), each now loved where he should, and each was beloved by whom she would. So the angry father was overruled. It was a day of forgiveness; it was Duke Theseus's wedding day.

"In the temple, by and by with us," he decreed, "these couples shall eternally be knit."

So Hermia and Lysander, Demetrius and happy Helena, winding arms and linking looks and smiles, followed the Duke and his company out of the glade, all spite and anger, all tears and heartbreak having faded into the semblance of a dream.

"When my cue comes, call me and I will answer."

Bottom awoke. He was alone. He scratched his head and, to his great relief, found that it was the proper head for Bottom. He shook it. It was indeed the self-same head he'd had for as long as he could remember. And yet there was a difference. There was a dream inside it, a dream of such brightness that Bottom, when he thought about it, shone like a star in boots. He smiled, and it was a rare smile, for Bottom, of all mortals, had walked, waking, in the kingdom of dreams.

"I will get Peter Quince to write a ballad of this dream," he decided. "It shall be called, 'Bottom's Dream', because it hath no bottom."

With that he went back to the town where his companions greeted him with relief and joy. Now the play could go forward, for Bottom was come among them again; and none but Bottom could ever have played Pyramus. Their pensions were certain and, for bully Bottom, as Flute the bellows-mender put it, "sixpence a day in Pyramus, or nothing."

That very day the Duke and his queen, and the two pairs of lovers, were married with due solemnity; and that night the tragedy of Pyramus and Thisbe was enacted before them with all the delicacy, wit and grace that Peter Quince and his company could command. Snug the joiner played the Lion to perfection, and Snout the tinker rose to great heights as the Wall. Starveling the tailor shone in the necessary part of the man in the moon; and Flute was a Thisbe to wring all hearts. But bully Bottom the weaver was best of all. He lived Pyramus, he died Pyramus, and lived again to take his bow, so powerfully that there was not, as they say, a dry eye in the house ... although whether the tears shed were of grief or laughter, none could say.

The play done, the married lovers went their ways to bed. For a little while the hall was empty; then Puck and Oberon and Titania, with all their gossamer train, came with glow-worm lamps to bless the house and bid goodnight.

Macbeth

Three old women out in a storm. But what old women, and what a storm! It banged and roared and crashed and rattled. The sky was quick with sudden glares, and the earth with sudden darknesses, darknesses in which wild images of rocks and frightened trees, like scanty beggars in the wind, leaped out upon the inner eye! And the old women! Ancient hags with backs hooped like question marks and their shabby heads nesting together, like brooding vultures . . .

"When shall we three meet again?" howled one, above the shrieking of the wind. "In thunder, lightning or in rain?"

"When the hurly-burly's done!" came an answer, lank hair whipping and half muffling the words. "When the battle's lost and won!"

"Where the place?"

"Upon the heath."

"And there to meet with Macbeth!"

The sky stared, then shut its eye . . . and when it looked again, the old women had gone. Had they been real or had they only been fantastic imaginings made up out of strange configurations of the rocks? Yet their words had been real enough. There was a battle being fought, and there was a man called Macbeth.

Macbeth! A giant of fury and courage, his sword arm whirling and beating like a windmill as he fought for his king against the treacherous enemies who sought to overturn the state. So tremendously did he fight that he made killing almost holy, and they say his blade smoked with traitors' blood.

A soldier from the battlefield, a gaudy, staggering patchwork of blood and gashes, came stumbling into the royal camp to tell the King of Macbeth's mighty deeds, of how he had come face to face with the worst of the King's enemies and, with one blow had "unseamed him from the nave to the chops, and fixed his head upon our battlements."

Amazed, good King Duncan listened to the eager account of his general's almost supernatural bravery and success; and, while he stood wondering how he might justly reward such service, news came of yet another victory. The treacherous Thane of Cawdor had been captured. The King sighed. The price of victory was high. He had once loved and trust Cawdor.

"Go pronounce his present death," he commanded sombrely; "and with his former title greet Macbeth . . . What he hath lost, noble Macbeth hath won."

He sent two messengers post-haste to greet the great general with his new title and with the heart-felt gratitude of his King.

The King's messengers travelled swiftly, but even before they has set out, other messengers were on their way to meet Macbeth, messengers who travelled as fast as thinking, messengers whose purpose was as dark as the King's was bright: the three old women of the storm.

It was towards evening. There was thunder in the air and little lightnings, like bright adders, wriggled across the sky. Here and there on the open heath naked trees seemed to hold up their hands in fear and dismay; and the three old women crouched and waited, still as stones. Presently there came a rolling and a rattling, as if a small thunder had lost its way and was wandering in the dark. The three old women nodded.

"A drum, a drum! Macbeth doth come!"

The drummer was Banquo, friend and companion-in-arms of Macbeth. The drum he carried had been salvaged from the battlefield, taken, perhaps, out of the cradling arms of some dead drummer-boy. Cheerfully he thumped it as he and mighty Macbeth strode on through the gathering night, their kilts swinging and their heads held high.

Suddenly they halted and the drum ceased like a stopped heart. Their way was barred. Three old women had appeared before them, three hideous old women who crouched and stared. For an instant, an uncanny fear seized the two warriors; then Banquo recovered himself. Imperiously he thumped on his drum and demanded:

"What are these, so withered and so wild in their attire?"

Silence. He thumped again.

"Live you?"

Their silence remained unbroken.

"Or are you aught that man may question?"

At this, the old women's eyes glinted, and slowly each raised a finger to her lips. Thus they crouched, like crooked answers awaiting only the right question, and the right questioner. They turned to the great, battle-stained figure of Macbeth. For the smallest moment, he hesitated; then commanded.

"Speak if you can! What are you?"

The right questioner. One by one they rose and greeted him.

"All hail Macbeth, hail to thee, Thane of Glamis!"

His rightful title, and Banquo thumped approval on his drum.

"All hail Macbeth, hail to thee, Thane of Cawdor!"

The drum faltered . . .

"All hail Macbeth, that shalt be King hereafter!"

King! The drum stopped. King! It seemed that another drum was beating. Macbeth could hear it, thudding and thundering in his ears. It was his furious heart! He trembled and grew pale, fearing that Banquo would hear the tell-tale sound. But Banquo was no more proof than he against the golden promise in the weird old women's words.

"If you can look into the seeds of time," he begged them eagerly, "and say which grain will grow and which will not, speak then to me . . ."

As before they answered, one by one.

"Lesser than Macbeth and greater," promised the first.

"Not so happy, yet much happier," promised the second.

"Thou shalt get kings though thou be none," promised the third.

"Stay, you imperfect speakers!" shouted Macbeth. "Tell me more!"

But even as he spoke, the weird sisters vanished, as abruptly as if, whispered Banquo, "The earth hath bubbles as the water has, and these are of them . . ."

It was then, as the two men stood, staring at one another and wondering if what they had seen and heard had been real, that the King's two messengers appeared, and the first of the weird sisters' prophecies came true. The King had made him Thane of Cawdor!

"What! Can the Devil speak true?" cried Banquo, involuntarily; and Macbeth's thoughts turned helplessly to the second prophecy: he would be King! If one had come true, why not the other? Dark thoughts filled his head, thoughts of how that prophecy might be made to come true. He tried to put them from him. He shook his head violently. "If Chance will have me King," he reasoned to himself, "why Chance may crown me without my stir."

But Chance proved as wayward as a woman, first offering, now denying. When he returned to the royal camp with the messengers, he heard King Duncan pronounce Malcolm, his son, as heir to the throne of Scotland. Chance had mocked him; all was lost. Then Chance offered again. The kindly King declared that he would travel to Inverness, and stay one night as the guest of his loyal and well-loved subject, Macbeth.

"Stars, hide your fires!" whispered Macbeth, as he set off ahead of the King to warn his wife to prepare for the royal night. "Let not light see my black and deep desires!"

The lady of the castle had a letter in her hand. Over and over again she read it as she paced back and forth across her tall chamber where the light came through a narrow window like a knife. Each time she crossed the beam, her red hair blazed, as if there was a furnace in her head. The letter was from her husband, Macbeth. It told of his meeting with the weird sisters, of their strange prophecies, and of how the first had already been fulfilled. She put the letter aside.

"Glamis thou art," she breathed, "and Cawdor, and shalt be what thou art promised . . ."

King! He must be King! But how was it to be brought about? Even as she wondered, a servant entered the room.

"What is your tidings?" she demanded.

"The King comes here tonight."

She caught her breath; she started violently.

"Thou'rt mad to say it!" she cried out, before she could prevent herself; for in that instant she knew that the messenger had announced the death of the King. She and her husband together would murder him.

When her husband came, wild and breathless from

his furious ride, she embraced him passionately; and, as they talked in low, rapid tones of the approaching King, she saw in his face that his thoughts were the same as hers. Yet perhaps they showed too plainly . . .

"Your face, my Thane," she warned him, "is as a book where men may read strange matters."

He nodded; then he faltered a little. Between the thinking and the doing of a deed, there was a line to be crossed. Though he was mighty in the trade of public blood, he shrank from private murder in the dark.

"We will speak further," he muttered.

But she would have none of it. Fate had promised him the crown, and the crown he would have.

"Only look up clear," she commanded. "Leave all the rest to me."

It was late afternoon when King Duncan, his two sons and his nobles, reached Inverness; and the lady of the castle, all smiles and bending like a flower, came out to greet them.

"Give me your hand," said the gentle King, and the lady, with welcome in her face and murder in her heart, gave the King her hand and drew him into her house.

That night, sounds of cheerful feasting filled the air; torches flamed in the stony passages and court-yards, making fantastic shadows of the hurrying servants, and the castle ran red with wine. But Macbeth, the host, was not at the feast. He had left the table in a mood of sudden horror at the thought of what he was to do. He stood alone in a courtyard, close against the wall.

"He's here in double trust," he whispered wretchedly: "first as I am his kinsman and his sub-ject, strong both against the deed; then as his host

119

who should against his murderer shut the door, not bear the knife myself."

"Why have you left the chamber?"

It was his wife. She had come in search of him. Her looks were fierce. He tried to avoid them.

"We will proceed no further in this business."

Furiously she turned on him for his cowardice.

"I dare do all that may become a man," he protested; "who dares do more is none."

Her eyes blazed, her scorn increased and stung him unbearably. He weakened. "If we should fail?"

"We fail!" she cried triumphantly. "But screw your courage to the sticking-place and we'll not fail!"

He stared at her, and she at him. He bowed his head. The matter was settled.

Past midnight. The feast was ended and the feasters all in bed. The torches were out and the castle was dark and quiet. Yet there was an uneasiness in the air, and sleep was restless. Two men crossed a court that was open to the black sky. One was Banquo, the other was Fleance, his son. A light approached.

"Who's there?"

It was the master of the house with a servant carrying a torch. His face was a rapid mingling of firelight and shadows, now seeming to scowl, now to grin, now plunged into utter gloom.

"I dreamt last night of the three weird sisters," murmured Banquo to his friend. "To you they have showed some truth."

"I think not of them," said Macbeth, and looked away. The friends parted. For a moment, Macbeth stared after Banquo and his son. Then he turned to his servant. "Go bid thy mistress," he ordered, "when my drink is ready she strike upon the bell."

The servant departed, and Macbeth waited, listening. Once again, horrible thoughts filled his head, and strange fancies . . .

"Is this a dagger which I see before me?" he breathed; for he did indeed seem to see such a weapon, eerily in the air, and it was thick with blood. Then, faintly, he heard the sound of a bell. Although he expected it, had been waiting for it, he started violently when it came.

"Hear it not, Duncan," he whispered, "for it is a knell that summons thee to heaven or to hell." Then, drawing his own dagger, he crept from the court like a ghost.

There was silence. Nothing stirred, nothing breathed. Then Lady Macbeth appeared. Her face was white; her eyes blazed with inward fire. She waited. Suddenly an owl screamed, and the night sighed. She stared towards the chamber where the King slept.

"He is about it."

A shadow moved. It was Macbeth.

"My husband!" she cried, and tried to embrace him. He pushed her aside.

"I have done the deed," he said, and stared down at his hands. He was holding two daggers: their blades and his hands were dripping with blood.

"This is a sorry sight," he said.

"A foolish thought, to say a sorry sight," cried she. But for once her words had no force for him. What he had done had put him out of her reach. To her, he had done no more than to kill an old man to get a crown; to himself, he had murdered sleeping innocence, he had murdered his own honour, he had killed his own soul. Already, he was a man apart.

"Why did you bring these daggers from the place?" she demanded. "They must lie there. Go . . ."

He shook his head. "I'll go no more. I am afraid to think what I have done; look on't again I dare not."

"Give me the daggers!" she exclaimed contemptuously. "The sleeping and the dead are but as pictures . . ."

She seized the daggers and left him. No sooner had she gone than there came a knocking on the outer gate. He shook and trembled and stared down at his murderer's hands. Lady Macbeth returned. Her hands were now as guilty as his.

"My hands are of your colour," she said, holding them up before him; "but I shame to wear a heart so white." She rubbed her hands together, and, as if comforting a child, said: "A little water clears us of this deed."

Then the knocking was heard again. It was loud and urgent. Husband and wife stared at one another – and fled.

It was Macduff who knocked at the gate, Macduff, the great Thane of Fife. He had come to rouse the King. His knocking had been so loud that all the castle had been awakened – all, that is, except for the King.

"I'll bring you to him," offered the master of the house. "This is the door," he said, gesturing with a white hand and a whiter smile. He stood aside and Macduff went in to the King.

He waited, at ease, it seemed, with the world. He waited for Macduff to cross the outer chamber; to reach the inner chamber; to open the door. He waited, still easy, until he heard the shout, the cry, the shriek of discovery, as Macduff saw what lay on the bed within. Then Macduff ran out. His looks were wild and frantic. The King was dead! He had been slaughtered as he slept!

"Murder and treason!" he shouted. "Banquo and Donalbain! Malcolm, awake!"

Murder and treason! The castle rocked. The very stones seemed to shake and glare. Murder and treason! Torches, like maddened fireflies, rushed hither and thither, throwing up faces, like sudden paintings of amazement and horror, as nobles and servants came tumbling upon the scene. Murder and treason! The King had been killed in the night! Who had done it? Why, his guards, of course, who else? Question them! Impossible! Macbeth had already stopped their tongues. Rage had overcome him and he had slaughtered them for the crime!

"Wherefore did you so?" demanded Macduff, a terrible suspicion awakening in his heart.

"Who can be wise, amazed, temperate and furious, loyal and neutral in a moment?" cried Macbeth. "No man."

The King's two sons looked fearfully to one another. Their father had been murdered. Would they be next?

"Where we are, there's daggers in men's smiles," muttered one.

"Therefore to horse," answered the other, "and let us not be dainty of leave-taking but shift away!"

They fled from the hall and from the castle, and from Scotland itself, leaving behind the dead King, the crown – and Macbeth.

The old women's prophecy was fulfilled. The grain they had spied in Macbeth's heart had grown and flourished in that dark place. He seized the crown and mounted the throne. He was King, and none dared oppose him: not murdered Duncan's sons, not great Macduff, nor even Banquo, who, of all men, knew enough to bring him down.

"Thou hast it now," murmured Banquo thoughtfully: "King, Cawdor, Glamis, all as the weird women promised; yet I fear thou playedst most foully for it . . ."

He was at Forres in the royal palace, soon after

Macbeth and his Lady had been crowned. There was to be a banquet that night. All the Scottish nobles, himself included, had been summoned to do homage to the new King. Banquo watched, but kept his thoughts to himself. This was partly caution, and partly because he also had been given a promise by the weird sisters. Though he would not be King himself, he would be father to kings.

"Ride you this afternoon?" inquired Macbeth, coming upon his old companion-in-arms, and fondly greeting him.

"Aye, my good Lord," answered Banquo, and confided that he would not be back till an hour or two after nightfall.

"Goes Fleance with you?"

"Aye, my good Lord . . ."

Macbeth nodded, and wished Banquo and his son Godspeed.

"Fail not our feast," he said and stared after Banquo long and deep. He had not forgotten the old women's prophecy to his friend; and the recollection of it festered in his heart.

A servant approached, bringing in two strange, muffled-looking men. They were grim fellows that the world had treated badly; and, in return, they were prepared to take their revenge upon the world – and upon Banquo, in particular.

They talked together and soon the matter was settled between them. The men departed, and Macbeth breathed harshly. "It is concluded!" he whispered. "Banquo, thy soul's flight, if it find heaven, must find it out tonight!" His friend and his friend's son were to be murdered that night.

"How now, my Lord? Why do you keep alone?"

Lady Macbeth approached the brooding King. Her face was worn, her eyes had lost their fire. She scarcely knew her husband any more. The deed he

124

had done had set him apart, and now they seemed to face different ways: she without, and he, within.

"What's done is done," she urged; for to her it was, but not so for him.

"We have scorched the snake, not killed it," he warned. Banquo and his son still lived.

"What's to be done?" she asked. He shook his head.

"Be innocent of the knowledge," he bade her, "dearest chuck, till thou applaud the deed . . ."

Banquo was not at the feast. All the world was there, laughing, smiling, jesting, drinking – but not Banquo. Macbeth, the royal host, walked among his guests in high good humour, found a place at table, sat down . . .

"We'll drink a measure," he proposed; when he saw a man appear in the doorway, a grim, muffled-looking man whose eye caught his, and who beckoned. Macbeth left the table and went to the man. He stood close, stared at him.

"There's blood upon thy face," he murmured.

"'Tis Banquo's then."

"Is he dispatched?"

"His throat is cut."

Macbeth nodded. And Fleance? What of the son? The man shook his head. The son had escaped. Dismay filled Macbeth's heart. Then he recovered himself. The worst, at least, was done. Banquo was dead. He dismissed the man and returned to the feast. He hesitated. The guests looked up at him.

"May it please your Highness sit?"

Macbeth frowned in puzzlement. "The table's full," he said.

"Here is a place reserved, Sir."

"Where?"

"Here, my good Lord."

He looked. He grew deathly white. He shook and

trembled till he could scarcely stand. He tried to speak. His voice was thick with dread.

"Which of you have done this?"

The place offered to him was filled. Banquo was sitting in it! Banquo, his head half off, and all painted with his life's blood! Grimly the ghost of the murdered man glared at his murderer.

"Thou canst not say I did it," groaned Macbeth; "never shake thy gory locks at me!"

Amazement seized the table as the guests saw the whitened King shake and stare and mutter at an empty stool. Urgently the Queen tried to calm the company, and still more urgently to calm her frantic husband.

"Why do you make such faces?" she whispered to him. "When all's done, you look but on a stool!"

Neither she nor anyone else could see what he could see. The ghost had come for him alone. Then it departed and briefly Macbeth recovered himself. But not for long. The gashed and bleeding spectre returned, and its dreadful looks drove the King into a frenzy.

The feast broke up in dismay, and the guests rose in confusion. The King was ill. What was wrong?

"I pray you speak not," cried the distressed Queen; "he grows worse and worse. Question enrages him. At once, good night. Stand not upon the order of your going; but go at once!"

Once alone, the Queen and King stared at one another across the ruins of the feast.

"It will have blood, they say," muttered Macbeth; "blood will have blood."

The Queen was silent.

"How sayest thou, that Macduff denies his person at our bidding?" he murmured, his thoughts turning to another enemy as he recollected that Macduff had failed to attend the feast.

"Did you send to him, Sir?"

"I heard it by the way," he said; "but I will send." Another crime, another murder . . . but did it matter any more? "I am in blood stepped in so far," he sighed, "that, should I wade no more, returning were as tedious as go o'er."

He shook his head. On the next day he would seek out those who had first set him on the dark and bloody path along which he had already travelled so far. The weird sisters.

"More shall they speak," he said; "for now I am bent to know by the worst means the worst."

They were waiting for him, even as once they'd waited before. They knew he would come. They waited in a dark room in a dark house in Forres, not very far from the royal palace; and, while they waited, they made ready.

"Double, double toil and trouble," they chanted, as they moved about a cauldron that smoked and reeked in the middle of the room; "fire burn and cauldron bubble." And into it they cast weird, unholy things.

Then they stopped.

"By the pricking of my thumbs," cried one, "something wicked this way comes!"

It was Macbeth. They stared at him, but did not speak. As before, they were answers awaiting a question.

"What is't you do?" he demanded, gazing at the cauldron.

"A deed without a name."

"Answer me to what I ask you."

"Speak," said one. "Demand," said another. "We'll answer," said the third. Then the first said: "Say if thou'dst rather hear it from our mouths or from our masters."

"Call 'em," commanded Macbeth; "let me see 'em."

The weird sisters obeyed. They poured blood into the cauldron, and presently there arose from it, wreathed in smoke and wearing a warlike helmet, a severed head. It hovered in the air and stared at Macbeth.

"Tell me, thou unknown power . . ." he began; but one of the sisters bade him only listen, as the apparition already knew what he had come to ask.

"Macbeth, Macbeth, Macbeth," it chanted; "beware Macduff! Beware the Thane of Fife!"

Then the head dissolved and its place was taken by another, even stranger sight. There floated in the air before him an infant, a little child all streaked with blood.

"Macbeth, Macbeth, Macbeth," it piped. "Be bloody, bold and resolute . . . for none of woman born shall harm Macbeth!"

He would have asked more, but this second apparition had already vanished, and its place was taken by a third. Another child. But now it was a child, wearing a crown and holding out the branch of a tree.

"Macbeth shall never vanquished be," this apparition told him, "until great Birnam Wood to high Dunsinane hill shall come against him."

"That will never be!" cried Macbeth, as the third apparition sank into smoky nothingness. What he had been told lifted up his heart and bewitched his spirits as if with wine! No man born of woman could ever harm him; and he would never fall till Birnam Wood came to Dunsinane. Such things could never happen, so he would never fall!

Yet there was still one thing he wanted to know. "Shall Banquo's issue ever reign in this kingdom?" he asked. "Seek to know no more," he was told. But he insisted, and, at length, he had his answer. Before his peering eyes the cauldron sank away and out of the thick air, silent and gleaming, there stalked a procession of kings. One by one they passed him by, each with a stare and each with a nod: five; six; seven; eight in all. And then came Banquo! Banquo, thick and clotted with blood. He pointed to the last of the kings who held up a glass; and in the glass were kings and more kings, stretching out into future time. Banquo smiled. Those kings to come were his!

Suddenly Macbeth was alone. Banquo, the kings and the weird sisters had vanished.

"Where are they?" he cried wildly. "Gone! Let this pernicious hour stand aye accursed in the calendar!"

Banquo's children would be kings. Macbeth would be barren. He himself was the beginning and the end of his line. But that was in the future. Present matters needed present action. That very day he sent men to murder Macduff.

But Macduff had forestalled him. He had fled to England and joined Malcolm, dead King Duncan's son. But he had left his wife and children behind.

"Where is your husband?" demanded Macbeth's murderers as they burst into her home.

She would not tell them; so they killed her, and all her children, and every living soul in the house.

In England, in peaceful, sunlit England, Malcolm and Macduff talked together of the sad plight of their own land that lay under the shadow of the tyrant King. Presently a messenger approached, a nobleman from Scotland. His looks were strange, his speech, halting.

"How does my wife?" asked Macduff.

"Why, well."

"And all my children?"

"Well too."

"The tyrant has not battered at their peace?"

"No. They were well at peace when I did leave 'em."

Then the messenger could keep back his terrible news no longer.

"Your castle is surprised, your wife and babes savagely slaughtered."

The great blow fell. Grief turned Macduff to stone. The world was empty for him now. Nothing remained but revenge.

Macbeth had gone to Dunsinane, and with him, like a painted shadow, went his Queen. Malcolm and Macduff were marching against him and he must needs prepare for war. He had no fear. No man born of woman could ever harm him, and he would not be vanquished till Birnam Wood should move and come to Dunsinane. Those were the promises of Fate. Yet he must be ready because Fate, he knew of old, needed a helping hand.

It was night in the castle of Dunsinane, and two figures stood close together in the dark hall. One was a doctor, the other a waiting-woman of the Queen.

"When was it she last walked?" asked the doctor, quietly.

"Since His Majesty went into the field."

"Besides her walking, and other actual perform-ances, what, at any time, have you heard her say?"

"That, sir, which I will not report after her."

"You may, to me . . ."

"Neither to you nor anyone," said the waiting-woman. "Lo you! Here she comes."

It was the Queen. She carried a taper and was in her night attire. Her eyes were open; but she was asleep.

"What is it she does now?" whispered the doctor. "Look how she rubs her hands."

"It is an accustomed action with her," murmured the woman, "to seem thus washing her hands. I have known her continue in this a quarter of an hour."

"Hark! She speaks," said the doctor eagerly; and he

and the waiting-woman listened intently to the strange mutterings of the Queen.

"Out, damned spot! Out, I say!" Her hands seemed to gnaw at each other like feverish mice, and the taper tipped and tilted, making wild shadows behind her. Then she cried out, in a voice that filled the listeners with horror: "Who would have thought the old man to have had so much blood in him?"

"She has spoke what she should not," whispered the waiting-woman. "I am sure of that."

Then her mistress, the Queen, still rubbing at her hands, complained that the smell of blood would not go; and she who had once told her husband that a little water cleared them of the deed, now cried out in anguish:

"All the perfumes of Arabia will not sweeten this little hand!" Then she drifted away. "To bed, to bed," she sighed. "What's done cannot be undone. To bed, to bed, to bed."

Malcolm and his army drew near. Already Birnam Wood was before them. It was thick and leafy.

"Let every soldier hew him down a bough," commanded Malcolm, "and bear it before him . . ."

Quickly it was done, and presently it seemed that Birnam Wood itself was moving towards Dunsinane.

Macbeth, secure in his prophecies, awaited the oncoming army. Suddenly he heard a cry, a desolate cry of women. Once, such a found would have alarmed him; but now he was past all feeling, past all fear. Wearily he asked the reason for the cry.

"The Queen, my Lord, is dead," he was told.

He shrugged his shoulders. "She should have died hereafter," he sighed. "There would have been a time for such a word. Tomorrow, and tomorrow, and tomorrow, creeps in this petty pace from day to day to the last syllable of recorded time . . ."

A messenger broke in upon his life-weariness, a messenger amazed and scarcely able to speak. He had been watching from a hill, and, as he watched, it had seemed to him that Birnam Wood was moving, moving towards Dunsinane.

"Liar and slave!" shouted Macbeth, rousing himself. Rage filled him, not against Malcolm, nor even against Macduff, but against the weird sisters, the Fates! They had deceived and entrapped him into destroying the great man that once he had been.

"They have tied me to a stake," he cried, "I cannot fly, but bear-like I must fight the course. What's he that was not born of woman? Such a one am I to fear, or none."

This last promise sustained him as he rushed from the castle to face his enemies. He fought like a giant, for who could harm him? His life, though he valued it at nothing, was charmed. Then, in the smoke of battle, he came face to face with Macduff.

"Of all men else I have avoided thee," he cried. "But get thee back; my soul is too much charged with blood of thine already."

"I have no words; my voice is in my sword!" shouted Macduff, and rushed upon him.

"I bear a charmed life," warned Macbeth, parrying his enemy's blows, "which must not yield to one of woman born!"

"Despair thy charm!" panted Macduff, his murdered wife and children ever in his thoughts. "Macduff was from his mother's womb untimely ripped!"

The last promise had been broken, and the last prophecy fulfilled. The end had come. Nothing now remained for him but to perish bravely, like the soldier that he had been.

"Lay on, Macduff!" he cried, his sword and shield

grasped firmly. "And damned be him that first cries, 'Hold, enough!'"

They fought, and Macduff killed Macbeth. Then he cut off his head and carried it, dripping, to Malcolm, the new King. He held it up on high, and its sightless glare bore witness to the double truth of Fate.

The best in classic and

Jane Austen

Elizabeth Laird

Beverley Naidoo   Roddy Doyle

Robert Swindells

George Orwell

Charles Dickens

Charlotte Brontë

Jan Mark

Anne Fine

Anthony Horowitz